"I loved this book! From the searing first sentence, it delivers on its promise to lay bare the common failings of the human heart. With great wisdom and practical help, *Overcoming Emotions That Destroy* unmasks the scary and oftentimes mysterious reality of anger, puts it under a literary microscope, and helps us deal with anger in a healthy way. It would be a wonderful sermon series, small group study, or husband/wife weekly devotional."

Gary Thomas, author of *Sacred Marriage* and *Holy Available*

"Practical . . . practical . . . practical! That's what makes this book so powerful. For anyone who *has* struggled . . . *is* struggling . . . or *will* struggle with the stranglehold of anger, this book is a must-read. Whether you—or someone you love—is a 'Spewer,' 'Stuffer,' or 'Leaker,' you'll find help and hope on every page."

June Hunt, founder and CEO, Hope for the Heart; author of *Counseling through Your Bible Handbook*

"Thank you, Chip and Becca, for giving us this timely resource. It is practical, biblical, and compellingly engaging. *Overcoming Emotions That Destroy* not only gives us the *what* and *why* of anger but it also shows us *how* to deal with this powerful emotion. My only complaint is that you didn't write it twenty years ago!"

Dr. Crawford W. Loritts Jr., speaker and author of *Leadership as an Identiy*

Overcoming Emotions
That Destroy

Overcoming Emotions That Destroy

Practical Help for Those Angry Feelings
That Ruin Relationships

Chip Ingram
Becca Johnson

BakerBooks

a division of Baker Publishing Group
Grand Rapids, Michigan

© 2009 by Chip Ingram and Becca Johnson

Published by Baker Books
a division of Baker Publishing Group
P.O. Box 6287, Grand Rapids, MI 49516-6287
www.bakerbooks.com

Published in association with Yates & Yates (www.yates2.com).

Paperback edition published 2010
ISBN 978-0-8010-7239-0

Printed in the United States of America

The Library of Congress has cataloged the hardcover edition as follows:
Ingram, Chip, 1954–
    Overcoming emotions that destroy : practical help for those angry feelings that ruin relationships / Chip Ingram and Becca Johnson.
        p.   cm.
    Includes bibliographical references.
    ISBN 978-0-8010-7213-0 (pbk.)
    1. Anger—Religious aspects—Christianity. I. Johnson, Becca Cowan, 1954–
II. Title.
BV4627.A5154 2009
248.8'6—dc22   2008054514

Unless otherwise noted, Scripture is taken from the HOLY BIBLE, NEW INTERNATIONAL VERSION®. NIV®. Copyright © 1973, 1978, 1984 by International Bible Society. Used by permission of Zondervan. All rights reserved.

Scripture marked KJV is taken from the King James Version of the Bible.

Scripture marked NRSV is taken from the New Revised Standard Version of the Bible, copyright 1989, Division of Christian Education of the National Council of the Churches of Christ in the United States of America. Used by permission. All rights reserved.

Scripture marked TNIV is taken from the Holy Bible, Today's New International Version™ Copyright © 2001 by International Bible Society. All rights reserved.

Chapter 15 contains material adapted from *Men's Work Facilitator's Guide: A Complete Counseling Plan for Breaking the Cycle of Male Violence*, copyright 1994, used by permission of the author, Paul Kivel. Further resources available at www.paulkivel.com.

11   12   13   14   15   16   7   6   5   4

Contents

Acknowledgments

Thank you to the many people who have shared both painful and victorious stories of their struggles with unwanted and seemingly uncontrollable emotions.

Thank you to my wonderfully supportive husband, Lloyd, and to my amazing children, who have put up with my anger more than I'd like to admit.

Thank you to Chip for your challenging, down-to-earth, inspiring teaching. Thank you also for walking in integrity and encouraging others to do so as well.

We would like to thank the many people who helped make this book a reality, from audio CDs to editing the written efforts to the published book. Thank you!

And finally, to the many who suffer from anger (their own or someone else's), may this book bring hope, help, and healing. We all hope this book will help both others and ourselves deal with anger in ways that honor God.

Dr. Becca Johnson

I would like to thank Dr. Becca Johnson for her initiative, hard work, and expertise as a psychologist, counselor, and published author. It was a privilege to team up with someone of her caliber, spiritually and educationally.

I would like to thank my good friend, Chris Tiegreen, for his editorial excellence and the Baker team of Chad Allen, Robert Hand, and Cheryl Van Andel for their cooperation and energy in both editorial and design.

This is my tenth book and there would not have been one without Yates and Yates. Thank you, Curtis and Sealy, for believing in me and the message God has given me.

Finally, a special thank you to my family for letting me share so many real stories of how God's grace has met us and grown us through our journey of *Overcoming Emotions That Destroy*.

Chip Ingram

PART 1

INTRODUCTION

1

Hope for Our Anger

If you let anger get the best of you, it will reveal the worst of you.

Her voice was trembling. From the moment she came on the air, I knew this was no ordinary call, and I would soon learn it was no ordinary story. I adjusted my earphones in the studio to get a clearer signal.

Between sobs of remorse and tears of joy, this young mother revealed a cycle of angry outbursts and physical abuse that had left her children recoiling and her overwhelmed with guilt and shame. But unlike the numbing headlines of today's newspaper or the bizarre tales of talk radio, this woman's story had a happy ending. She was calling to say thank you. She had learned to bring her anger under control; she wasn't yelling at her children anymore, and the physical abuse had stopped.

Her gratitude was in response to a series of messages titled "Overcoming Emotions That Destroy." Her voice quickened with excitement as she shared key insights that God had used to transform her and her family.

As I drove home later that afternoon, it dawned on me just how pervasive this problem of anger is, along with all its accompanying emotions, such as guilt, shame, and frustration. I hadn't given it much thought until then, but as I crawled along on the crowded expressway, I distinctly remembered a conversation I'd had after teaching the same material earlier in the year.

A well-dressed, distinguished man with a deep tan, white hair, and gold watch was sitting with his attractive wife in church one Sunday. At the close of the service, he grabbed my elbow as I was leaving the auditorium. He directed me through the crowded room to a semiprivate nook and then broke into one of the biggest grins I've ever seen. I recognized his face as a regular at our church, but I didn't know him personally. Leaning toward my left ear, he said, "I can't tell you how much this teaching series is helping me. I'm an exploder. I've vomited my anger on everyone around me for twenty-five years. I've wrecked relationships, almost ruined my marriage, and hated myself in the process. I've tried everything and had all but given up. But last week when you said that anger is a secondary emotion and that it's a symptom, not the real problem, the lights came on! It was one of the most amazing insights of my entire life."

As I strained to hear this man's story over the noise of the room, I couldn't help but see his wife taking notice of our conversation. With my ear tilted to hear him more clearly and my eyes looking back toward his wife, I caught a quick smile from her that seemed to say, "I never dreamed he'd change, let alone that he'd be talking with you about something that has been so carefully hidden from the public for so many years."

Reflecting further, my mind began an informal inventory of letters, incidents, and private conversations I've had since this "Overcoming Emotions That Destroy" series was presented at our church and on the radio.

I recalled a letter from a middle-aged woman that about knocked me off my feet. She was not the kind of person you'd expect to have significant, unresolved issues swirling in her soul for years. But after describing some deep disappointments with her husband and extended family, she revealed a long, dark struggle with depression. Counseling and medication had helped her cope, but she was never far from feeling worthless and discouraged. She had experienced a breakthrough, however, as she listened to the teaching tapes related to anger. Even though she had heard that 90 percent of depression could be related to unresolved anger, she assumed that didn't apply to her. She was, in fact, very quiet and compliant and had never yelled or exploded at anyone. Anger certainly was not a problem area for her—or so she thought. What she learned through the series, however, was that she was a "Stuffer." She had been taught that anger was wrong and had learned to "bottle it up," to shove it down deep inside. She thought that stuffing her anger was a godly and proper response. Her letter went on to detail a journey of uncovering piles of unresolved anger and learning to process and express that anger appropriately. To her amazement and joy, she now had freedom from her lifelong depression.

Like pieces of a jigsaw puzzle fitting together in my mind, these responses were helping me begin to understand how our failure to understand anger wreaks havoc in our lives. I knew it was a hot issue when I first taught the series, but these responses—both in their variety and sheer number—caused me to rethink the importance of this subject. As a result, I decided about two years after first teaching it to revise the material and teach it again at our church. This overwhelmingly confirmed what I had learned in the past, but now with greater trust and deeper relationships, the feedback was even more honest.

A close friend approached me at about the midpoint of this teaching series and, rolling his eyes, said, "Wow, do I have some work to do!"

"What do you mean?" I asked.

"Well, I learned today that I'm a 'Leaker.' It hit me why I'm so frustrated with the sexual dimension of our marriage. My wife does things that bug me, but rather than openly and honestly tell her what they are and how I feel, I unconsciously record them, put them on a mental scorecard, and then 'leak' my anger toward her on 'safer playing fields.' Chip, you can't believe how sarcastic I've become over the years and how I put her down and tease her about stuff all the time. I manage to work the things that bug me into the conversation, but I do it in a half-joking manner so that if she gets steamed, I can laugh it off and tell her I was only joking. When you talked about leaking our anger and how anger puts a barrier in the intimate aspect of a relationship, it was like someone crawled inside my head and allowed me to see the real issue."

So how about you? Did your heart resonate with one of the people I just described? Could you or someone you love have an anger problem that's resulting in emotions that destroy relationships, produce guilt, and rob you of joy? If so, do you realize there's hope? Did you know that just as these real people found real help, you don't have to be a slave to anger or any related emotions that destroy? You may not have considered that anger issues go way beyond a bad temper or an occasional blowup; understanding what anger is, how it works, and how to deal with it positively could be the key to overcoming chronic depression, sexual frustration, and relational breakdowns. In fact, anger may not have to be your enemy at all; it can be harnessed to help you grow personally, relationally, and spiritually like you've never imagined. If all this sounds too good to be true, let me assure you we're offering no magic pills or quick, simplistic solutions to complex problems. We do, however, have a stream of testimonies that show how knowing the truth about anger can be liberating, both personally and in relationships with others.

The stories I have shared are but a tiny sampling of the responses we've received while teaching this material over the last decade. I tell them not because I have some extraordinary ability to teach, but because millions of people are held hostage by their anger and don't know how to deal with it. In many cases, they don't even realize they're held hostage.

This book has grown out of our hearts' desire to see God help others. The greatest teacher in the world said, "You will know the truth, and the truth will set you free" (John 8:32). This book is designed to get at the truth about our anger so that you and those you love can be set free.

Have you ever . . . ?

- Have you ever done something you wished you hadn't when you were angry?
- Have you ever said something when you were angry you wish you could take back?
- Have you ever made a bad decision when you were angry?
- Have you ever ruined a friendship, a marriage, a family relationship, a ministry relationship, or a business relationship because of anger?
- Have you ever seen a person hurt because of someone's anger—physically, emotionally, or psychologically?

It's amazing what we do when we're angry. We may blow up in haste at a boss: "I'm tired of being treated this way! You can take this job and shove it. I'm out of here!" Then a little later on the phone: "Uh, honey, I lost my job. Yeah, I know we have a lot of bills. No, my boss really doesn't want to talk about it anymore."

Or we may shut down in silence: "Honey, what's wrong? Please tell me. Please talk to me. Did I do something wrong? What's eating at you?"

Or we may gossip and get back indirectly: "Did you hear what she did? Can you believe it? I wouldn't want to judge, but I think what she did was ungodly and foolish. I wouldn't share this if I wasn't concerned. Of course, *I'm* not affected personally."

We make a lot of bad decisions when we're angry. When we get out a sword of anger, we cut people by shutting them out or by knocking them over. Many of the scars we inflict, whether directly or indirectly, are not easily healed.

> **We make a lot of bad decisions when we're angry.**

Solomon, an ancient king known for his wisdom, wrote many sayings. "A hot-tempered person commits many sins" (Prov. 29:22 TNIV), he warned. When angry, we are more apt to do something wrong. We often have wrong reactions and do dumb deeds. We say things that shouldn't be said, we lash out and hurt people, we do things we abhor, we build up fortresses to keep others out, or we project our anger onto undeserving souls. We generally react in ways that intensify rather than relieve our anger. We end up inviting either self-hatred and shame (internalized anger) or resentment and bitterness (externalized anger) into our hearts.

Here is a list of common anger triggers:

We feel categorized or stereotyped.
We feel trapped.
We feel unfairly treated.
We feel blamed.
We feel ignored, misunderstood, insignificant, belittled, or put down.

We feel entitled to something and don't get it. Our expectations aren't met.

We are given unsolicited advice. We feel that someone has treated us in a condescending way.

We are teased insensitively.

We are criticized.

Someone hasn't respected our limits.

We are given ultimatums or threats.

We are kicked, pushed, slapped, or hit.

Our space or territory has been invaded.

We don't feel safe.

We feel self-pity.

We don't admit our imperfections.

Where Are You with Anger?

Have you been scared and scarred by the anger, rage, screaming, and abuse of other people? Are your memories full of anger-filled moments? It's painful to be on the receiving end of someone's emotional outburst.

Or have you found yourself more often on the giving end? Do you need help controlling and containing your anger? Do you need to confess, "When I get angry, I blow. I've hurt those around me, those I love. I'm out of control! *Help!*"?

Do you stuff your anger and pretend you don't have a problem because you keep it from showing? Have you held your feelings in for years, developing ulcers, headaches, intestinal problems, and other kinds of physical ailments?

Do you assume blame when you or others get mad? "Whenever I feel angry or anyone is angry with me," a woman shared, "I assume it's my fault. I try to figure out what I did wrong, what I did to make the other person mad, or where I was at fault." Do you feel all anger is your fault?

Do you automatically blame others? When you're mad or someone is mad at you, do you assume, without question, that the other person is to blame? Do you tend to point your finger at external things (other people, places, and things) rather than look for internal reasons (your own ego, pride, hurt, or selfishness) for your anger?

Do you find yourself avoiding people when you're mad? Do you seek ways to get back indirectly?

Whether we blame ourselves or others, whether we express or repress, whether we avoid or attack, anger still exists. It doesn't go away. It just comes out in different ways. A client shared that even though he's generally good at controlling his anger, keeping it bottled up, "Every once in a while I blow up. And when I do, it's pretty bad—as if I've saved it [the anger] up for a long time."

> It doesn't go away. It just comes out in different ways.

This book is for everyone. It is for those who: (1) feel a need to deal with their anger; (2) need help communicating anger effectively; (3) want to move on and let go of the past; (4) find a string of broken, bleeding relationships due to their angry outbursts; (5) feel isolated and/or lonely because of their anger; (6) are unhappy; and (7) feel out of control.

Whom Can You Trust?

We hope by now your heart is stirred, your ears are perked, and somewhere in your skeptical heart you are saying, "It sounds good, but where does this advice come from? Who are Chip Ingram and Becca Johnson, and why should I trust what they have to say?"

In a world full of self-help, "promise people anything" to sell a book atmosphere, we think that's a valid question that deserves an honest answer. Chip is the teaching pastor of *Living on the Edge* radio ministry, former president of Walk Thru the Bible, and former senior pastor at Santa Cruz Bible Church. He has done graduate work in education, psychology, and theology and has a passion to help people take the truth and put it into practice in ways that impact their whole lives and relationships. He is married and has four grown children.

Dr. Johnson is a licensed psychologist and author of books on guilt and child abuse. She is a wife, mother of four and "missionary-at-large," providing counselor training around the world. Her life's work is to encourage people to work through painful experiences and emotions in order to more fully enjoy God's love. Her desire is to help the hurting heal with God's hope. She brings a wealth of invaluable insight, education and experience.

Above all, we are both "fellow strugglers" in this arena of anger. We have both been unfairly treated, had plans thwarted, been let down, felt rejected, and been wrongfully accused. We have also yelled; made big mistakes; been prideful, self-centered, and self-righteous; and been rightfully accused. We have cried and lamented, whined and pouted. We struggle with anger in our relationships with our spouses, our children, family, friends, and colleagues. We both have more firsthand experience with anger than we care to admit. We know anger from the receiving as well as the giving end.

This book is simple, but not simplistic. It is practical, but not just a list of self-help tools to merely manage your anger. It is theologically rooted and biblically accurate, but not preachy or religiously trite. It is psychologically sound, but not filled with psychological jargon. Our goal is to help you! As stated before, we promise no magic formulas, no easy shortcuts, and no soft answers for hard questions. But we do promise clear, practical, accurate information that, if applied faithfully, will teach you how to stop wasting your anger and start harnessing it as one of the most powerful change agents and motivational factors in your life.

This book seeks to help answer these questions:

- When is my anger valid?
- When is my anger destructive either to me or to others?
- How do I express anger?
- What does God say about anger?
- What does God recommend regarding anger?
- When should/shouldn't I get angry?

It's okay to skip around this book, reading the parts most applicable to your needs. We've purposefully tried to make short, easy-to-read chapters that you can complete in about five to ten minutes each. We have also included lots of charts and information for quick summary and reference. Our hope and prayer is that you will attempt to learn, apply, change, and/or get help.

In this book, we also hope you will be able to:

- identify the unhealthy ways you respond to anger;
- uncover the feelings underneath your anger;
- choose God-given, emotionally healthy ways to deal with anger;
- incorporate practical suggestions and exercises in dealing with anger into your life;
- deepen your understanding of God and his purpose for anger; and
- rejoice in God's anger-abatement plan.

The Benefits of Dealing with Anger

When we learn to effectively experience and deal with our anger, we find that our relationships are healthier, our work is less stressful, and our lives are more enjoyable. We have fewer diseases and physical complaints, and we have less need to control, avoid, or defend ourselves in relationships. Instead of taking our anger out negatively on ourselves or on those around us, we learn to direct it in ways that are helpful rather than harmful. Rather than blame ourselves, God, our parents, the boss, coworkers, our spouses, our children, or friends, we can learn to constructively identify the source and nature of our feelings.

Anger has great power for both good and bad and should be dealt with in ways that are constructive rather than destructive. We need to face our anger and force ourselves to deal with it. As we confront our anger, we develop clearer boundaries in our relationships; we experience open, honest communication; and we are better in tune with our own needs and desires.

The Bottom Line

Anger is a pervasive problem, but there's hope in learning how to deal with it.

Questions to Consider

1. Do you or someone you know have a problem with anger?
2. What have you/they done about it?
3. What has worked or been helpful in bringing about positive change? What hasn't worked?

Action Steps to Take

- Think about a time when you got angry, and identify as specifically as you can how you should have responded differently.
- Ask someone you trust to tell you about a time when they saw you get angry. Ask them to tell you how they think you express anger and when you are most likely to become angry.
- On an index card, write a few statements regarding what you hope to learn from this book. Then sign the card and put it in a conspicuous place where you will see it often.

2

Understanding Our Anger

Anger is never without a reason,
but seldom with a good one.

—Benjamin Franklin

It has the power to transform a tenderhearted mother into a harsh critic who destroys the dignity of her child.

It has the power to turn passionate lovers into cold, calculated, critical marriage partners who do only the bare minimum, only what's absolutely necessary to coexist in the same house. It can turn good friends into annoying antagonizers.

It has the power to turn a festive family gathering into a gut-twisting, name-calling, side-taking, no-holds-barred family feud that rarely, if ever, gets resolved.

It has the power to turn caring, concerned parents into neck-bulging, vein-popping, screaming adults who say the same thing over and over again into the blank faces of their children.

It has the power to turn a calm, quiet, conscientious, longtime employee into an automatic-weapon-carrying maniac who goes floor to floor in an office building spraying bullets everywhere, killing and maiming innocent people, simply because he was let go from his job.

What is it that has this kind of power? Unfortunately, it's not some rare disease or strange psychological disorder. It resides in your life and in ours, in your heart and in ours. It's something we can't escape.

It's the power of our emotions. Designed by God to allow us to respond to and enjoy our world, emotions also have the influence to get us off track and out of whack, being used in ways we never intended. God intended for our feelings to be helpful, positive, and a blessing. One helping professional wrote, "Emotions were never meant to be destructive or harmful. In fact, the opposite is true . . . emotion is a physiological sensation . . . to satisfy or warn of a human need."[1] But too many times, in too many ways, with too many unresolved feelings in our hearts, these emotions have the power to ruin families, break up marriages, destroy friendships, decimate workplaces, and divide ministries.

> It is a common, unavoidable, inescapable, God-given emotion.

We believe that one of the most potentially damaging emotions is anger, an emotion that both empowers and plagues every one of us. It is a common, unavoidable, inescapable, God-given emotion. In these pages we'll take a look at what the Bible and psychology say about it. You may be surprised to discover that psychological advice and research affirm biblical truth. But before we begin, we want to ask you to ponder a few questions.

Have you ever gotten mad because . . .

- someone cut in line or cut you off while driving?
- someone misunderstood what you said?
- someone ignored your feelings?
- of a relationship breakup?
- of feeling trapped, smothered, controlled?

- you feel like a failure?
- someone broke your trust?
- of past abuse?
- someone lied to you?
- you had to wait a l–o–n–g time in the checkout line at the store?
- your children were not obeying?
- the waitress was slow or brought the wrong food?
- you stubbed your toe?
- you find out too late that you're out of toilet paper?
- the line to use the public restroom is *very, very* long?
- your spouse forgot to call and was very late?
- the clothes you wanted to wear are still in the laundry hamper, not yet washed?
- your spouse has been unfaithful?
- you ran out of time and weren't able to get some things done you needed to?
- you drove all the way across town only to find the store was out of the item you needed?
- the kids continually and relentlessly demand your time?
- you forgot to do something you were supposed to?
- you have no time for yourself?
- someone said something harsh and insensitive?
- a store clerk was rude?
- you were in a hurry and you hit all red lights?
- your boss doesn't appreciate you the way you think he or she should?
- someone tracked dirt into the freshly cleaned house?
- the driver in front of you is going so-o-o-o-o s–l–o–w?
- someone close to you died?

You get the point. We get angry. We get angry at little things, and we get angry at big things. We get angry at people, and we get angry at situations, institutions, God, and ourselves.

What Is Anger?

It's hard to put a finger on exactly what anger is, but everyone who has experienced it—in other words, *everyone*—knows how it feels. As author Tim Jackson states,

> At times, anger can feel like an inner fire. It hits you in the gut. You see red and feel hot and sweaty. Your stomach churns, your blood pressure rises, your breathing rate increases as if you're laboring under a heavy weight. Outwardly, your body responds to the internal activity with a flushed appearance. You perspire, your nostrils may flare, and your jaw tightens. Many people describe their experience of anger as their blood boiling. On the other hand, anger can be experienced as compliance on the outside while resentment and hostility run just beneath the surface. The little boy who complies with his teacher's request to sit down may still be standing on the inside.[2]

That's a good description of how we experience anger. But what is it? Anger has been defined in different ways by sociologists, psychologists, theologians, and others. It has been considered a natural, adaptive response to our environment. The *American Heritage Dictionary* calls it "a strong feeling of displeasure or hostility." Don Richmond, a colleague, describes it as "both a divine and human emotion which is aimed at the rectification of wrong and must be wisely expressed and carefully monitored." And it's true—anger needs to be expressed *and* monitored.

Synonyms for *angry* include: *enraged, furious, indignant, mad, seething, infuriated, aggravated, irate, annoyed, bothered, frustrated, huffy, inflammatory, irascible, provoked, red hot, riled up, short-* or *quick-tempered, ticked off, peeved,* and *hot.*

In our opinion, anger is an emotion that in and of itself is not inherently good or bad. It has both positive and negative qualities. Does that surprise you? Anger isn't bad or wrong. It's a signal that something is uncomfortable, wrong, or undesirable. It's a feeling of intense displeasure, disdain, or discontent. But anger in itself, contrary to the view of many, is not bad.

We define anger as a charged, morally neutral, emotional response of protective preservation. Those words were chosen carefully. Anger is charged, full of energy. It gets our juices flowing, our hearts pounding, our minds racing. It's also morally neutral. It's neither good nor bad; it's simply an emotion, a feeling.

Anger has potential for great use and great misuse. It can be motivating, helpful, and constructive, but it can also be damaging, harmful, and destructive. When it motivates us to fight against injustices and to correct attitudes and behaviors we perceive to be wrong, it can be very healthy. Most of us think we should be angry less, but we would suggest that many of us need to be angry more—for the right reasons and in the right way.

> **Anger has potential for great use and great misuse.**

Anger's basic goal is to protect and preserve. When we feel threatened, whether emotionally or physically, it activates our survival instincts. Though it can motivate us to preserve and protect what's right, it is unfortunately often used to preserve and protect *us* in unhealthy ways that actually keep us from facing the real problem. If you don't want people near you, get angry—scream at them or shut them out. That works. If you don't want to be vulnerable, if you don't want to share the deep issues of your life, if you don't want to struggle with inner things that God wants to work out, just shut down or spew out. If that doesn't work, withdraw, be sullen, pout, be late, procrastinate, jab, be sarcastic, be critical, be faultfinding. It all works.

Anger communicates through its intensity, and it communicates beyond the spoken word. Our job is to decipher what our anger is really expressing. Here's a brief summary of what anger is and is not:

Anger is:	Anger is not:
☐ a tool of communication	☐ bad
☐ a morally neutral emotion	☐ a sin
☐ a signal of underlying emotions	☐ dangerous

The Good Side of Anger

When most of us look at this chart, we balk at the "Anger is not" column. We've been exposed only to the negative side of anger and, as a result, don't know how to recognize and channel healthy, appropriate anger for good. I (Chip) remember getting really angry at a laundromat years ago. A young mother and her toddler daughter were there while I was waiting for a load of clothes to dry, and I'd enjoyed watching and interacting with the little girl as she played. But the mother got annoyed at something the girl did and immediately turned into an angry beast. She picked her daughter up by one arm, banged her against a dryer, slammed her into a chair, and screamed in her face.

I was furious. I told the woman that her behavior was disgraceful and unacceptable, and I determined to do something about it. After strongly confronting her, I went to county authorities who, as it turns out, had too much red tape and not enough resources to deal effectively with situations like this. I suddenly found myself on an action committee—the Child Welfare Board. It was one of those situations where those who express interest get nominated to help. Eventually, our church and several others joined together to provide resources and temporary shelter for distressed families. It turned into one of the most effective programs in our community. In this case, my anger was appropriate and very fruitful. In fact, it would have been wrong not to get angry at such blatant injustice. When we see things that anger God, it's right for us to feel the same as he does—and to handle it productively.

But this isn't simply my personal experience. Do you remember when Moses came down from the mountain after he received the Ten Commandments? Instead of waiting on and trusting in God, the people of Israel threw a party to a golden calf they'd made while Moses was busy with God. It was immorality gone berserk. What did Moses do? He got mad. He felt righteous anger! He had the guts to stand up alone against a million people. He took those tablets, threw them down, and said (I'm paraphrasing), "Let's line up. Everyone on God's side over here. Whoever wants to keep up this nonsense, over there." He dealt with it and brought about positive change.

And what about David when he was just a young boy? The Philistines were taunting and teasing Israel's people about their God. Unfortunately, the king, the warriors, and David's brothers all became accustomed to it. They were hearing things that no one should ever say about God. Every morning, Goliath would say, in effect, "You know, your God is a wimp and so are you. He's nothing." David answered (paraphrasing again), "Hey king, brothers, and you warriors, is everyone going to let that big baboon talk about our God like that?" They sheepishly responded, "Well, he's kind of big." David replied, "I don't care how big he is. That giant is not going to talk about my God that way. Give me a slingshot; I'll take him on!" Out of this anger, he chose to do something significant. His anger led him to act.

Even Jesus got mad when he saw the temple being used like a shopping mall where people made money from religion. The temple was designed to be a place of adoration and worship of the Most Holy God, not a money-making industry. His anger was a righteous, motivating anger. He said, "My Father's house will not be like this." He threw over some tables, made a whip with some cords, and drove the people and animals out, restoring a sense of holiness to the place of worship.

Anger can be a powerful emotion and a positive motivator.

Good Anger Is Good

You need to get angry. We all need to get angry more. We need to pray, "God make me angry about things that make you angry." When's the last time you got mad about something that was wrong? When was the last time you did something rather than just complaining about it?

Anger can be used positively for emotional and physical protection, to communicate feelings, to motivate and energize others, to maintain social order, and to train young children. It's okay to be angry. We need to be sure, however, that we get angry about the right things and respond in the right way. Many of us may start off with the right reason and the right motives but end up either with the wrong actions or with a completely overblown response. Though we may be motivated by a good cause, we may still respond in ways that are damaging and painful. Anger can be a powerful and positive motivator, but because it's such a volatile emotion, it can quickly turn in negative directions and get us in incredible trouble.

> It's okay to be angry. We need to be sure, however, that we get angry about the right things and respond in the right way.

The Bad Side of Anger

Though anger can be very positive and constructive, it can also be negative and destructive. It can be an unhealthy emotional response to protect us from real or perceived hurt, frustration, or personal attack. Proverbs 29:22 says, "An angry man stirs up dissension, and a hot-tempered one commits many sins." Anger can stir up trouble and keep it brewing, stewing, and simmering. The result? We make mistakes and misunderstand. We blame and belittle. We become mean and malicious. We demolish and demean. We become spiteful and sinful. When you and I are angry, we tend to sin a lot. Anger that is not bridled nor righteously motivated can become a dangerous force. Our energy becomes focused on persevering and protecting our pride and our interests. When this happens, our anger becomes self-centered and self-righteous.

When a friend accused me (Becca) of wrong motives several years ago, I got mad. How dare he say such things? I immediately began to justify my actions. I became self-absorbed in my cause and self-righteous in my attitude. It didn't take long for my spouse to take me aside and lovingly point out the sinfulness of my behavior. I was wrongfully accusing my accuser—doing the same thing he did to me. I acted wrongly when wronged.

When we get angry, verbal abuse erupts, physical assaults increase, emotional attacks escalate, and character assassinations multiply.

Anger is a problem when it:

1. is used in the wrong ways,
2. occurs too frequently,
3. lasts far too long, and
4. results in inappropriate behavior.

Anger needs to be expressed at the right times, in the right ways, for the right reasons, in the right degree, and for the right length of time. The potential for misfiring on any of these points is great. Our feelings can often take over our better judgment, causing us to react disproportionately to the situation. In many cases, it can turn us into beasts, as I (Chip) witnessed in the laundromat with the abusive mother. But even when our reaction isn't that extreme, it can be misplaced—and very damaging.

Hanging on to Anger

Though Bill was in his fifties and his father had passed away a number of years earlier, he still clung tightly to his long-held and deep-seated anger at his dad. That's why he came to counseling. In the first few sessions, he shared many of the reasons for his anger. I told him that those events would make most people mad—but that it would be in his best interests to give up the anger and move on. "What are you getting out of staying angry?" I asked. "Why have you hung on to it?" Fortunately, Bill listened as I explained why many people have a hard time letting go of offenses.

While most of us would agree that we should get rid of destructive, counterproductive anger, many of us, whether consciously or subconsciously, tend to keep it around. We use it vicariously for numerous reasons that directly and indirectly benefit us. We may say we want to get rid of it but have actually found ways to use it to our advantage.

How do we do this? Some of us discover how effective anger is in controlling others, so we use it as a tool to orchestrate our relationships and environments. We find that we can use it to get others to do what we want. We use it to manipulate and maneuver those around us.

Some find that getting anger out makes them feel better, so they vomit it on others to achieve inner peace. Others who are uncomfortable in social settings find anger useful in keeping people at a distance. When people are alienated, there is no need to work things out.

Anger can also be useful in keeping us from facing the deeper issues in our lives. When we focus on our anger, we don't have to deal with the root problems. It functions like a shield to hide our deeper wounds.

For those feeling powerless or insecure, anger can become a powerful, domineering, intimidating weapon. Some find that keeping people at a distance also keeps away their scrutiny, criticism, and confrontations. Many have found that holding on to anger helps avoid conflict because people stay away. People generally steer clear of those they know will blow.

Many hang on to anger as a weapon of revenge. Letting go of it feels like letting a person off the hook. Others keep using anger in spite of experiencing negative consequences because they view change as too difficult and demanding. They need encouragement and energy to change as well as a better attitude. Similarly, some keep anger around simply because it's familiar. They fear the unknown and what might take anger's place if they dealt with it.

Some find that anger gives them a "high." They are energized and invigorated by the physiological and emotional sensations that accompany it. And anger helps others feel morally superior. They see it as righteous rather than *self*-righteous anger, justified rather than prideful.

Here's a summary of the many reasons we knowingly or unknowingly use anger for our benefit.

We keep anger around:

- to control or manipulate others
- to regurgitate negative emotions
- to relieve stress
- to keep people at a safe distance
- to avoid having to face our deeper, more painful problems
- to draw attention away from real issues
- to hide deeper hurts

- to feel dominant, powerful, intimidating
- to take revenge
- to avoid scrutiny
- to avoid conflict
- to avoid change
- to avoid having to face the unknown
- to feel superior to others

Do you find yourself using anger for one of these reasons? Have you found it useful in any of these detrimental ways? Warning: such actions are harmful to your emotional health! It's hard to get rid of anger when we're holding it tightly.

Keep the Baby, but Throw Out the Dirty Bathwater!

Most of us are familiar with the saying, "Don't throw out the baby with the bathwater." It also applies to anger. We aren't saying get rid of all anger, only that anger that is destructive and harmful. Part of the problem, to extend the analogy, is that it's often hard to distinguish the baby from the bathwater! What part of anger should we keep, and what part needs to be discarded? We'll try to answer these questions in the later chapters. For now, let's begin by looking at the three common ways in which we respond to anger. As we proceed, see if you can identify your anger profile.

The Bottom Line

Anger is a charged, morally neutral emotional response of emotional preservation. It can be a positive motivator for good or a negative motivator for bad.

Questions to Consider

1. What makes you angry?
2. When and where is it okay to feel angry?
3. In what ways do you tend to misuse anger? What perceived benefits do you get from keeping your anger? What do you gain from hanging on to it?
4. Has anger ever turned you into a beast? If so, what damage did it cause?

Action Steps to Take

- From your experience, think of an example that fits each item on the following list:

  Anger is a problem when it . . .
  1. is used in the wrong ways;
  2. occurs too frequently;
  3. lasts far too long; and
  4. results in inappropriate behavior.

  Describe what the appropriate response would have been in each example.
- Go back to the list of the many ways we benefit by hanging on to anger. Place a check next to those you tend to use. Stop and ask God to help you to be willing to let go of the anger.

PART 2

THE MANY FACES OF ANGER

3

Why We Respond
the Way We Do

Hot heads and cold hearts never solved anything.
—Billy Graham

Most people wrongly assume that those who explode are the only ones who have a problem with anger. In fact, you may be reading this book hoping to help that hothead you're married to, work with, or are trying to parent. But keep your antennae up—there might be a moment of insight and help awaiting you in the pages that follow. Anger can be expressed in several emotionally unhealthy ways that are different and distinct.

According to one survey, 23 percent of Americans admit to openly expressing (exploding) their anger, while approximately 40 percent report that they hold it in or hide it. Almost one-fourth (23 percent) confess to having hit someone in anger, while 17 percent admit they have destroyed the property of someone with whom they were mad.[1]

What do you do with anger? How do you tend to deal with it?

The Many Ways We Respond When Angry

Listed below you will find the most common ways we respond to anger. Read the list slowly. Then, with as much honesty as you can muster, place a light check mark in pencil next to the ways that most characterize your response to anger.

Shut down

Assert power and authority

Become pushy or aggressive

Yell, scream, shout, slam

Belittle (demean, slander)

Intimidate others

Become depressed

Isolate yourself

Alienate others

Suppress your feelings

Repress

Regress

Become fearful

Grab, hit, push, beat, kick, slap, or throw things

Become defensive

Become prideful and arrogant

Become withdrawn

Become self-righteous

Lie

Cuss

Withhold affection

Whine

Put others down

Roll your eyes

Spew out

Threaten others

Become hostile and/or violent

Blame others

Feel shame

Manipulate others

Experience self-hatred

Cover up your feelings

Pretend you do not feel the way you do

Rationalize and/or justify your actions or feelings

Make excuses

Become discouraged, despondent, and depressed

Gossip, slander

Become selfish and self-centered

Minimize how your anger affects others

Deny your feelings

Feel self-pity

Become critical and cynical

Become sarcastic

Give the "silent treatment"

Cry

42

Point your finger, or flip the middle finger	Groan
	Give ultimatums
Frown	Shrug your shoulders
Shake your fist and/or head	Sneer

Did you find yourself in the list? We sure did—several times. When we get mad, we respond in different ways at different times, depending on the situation. Sometimes we become critical, other times we gossip, and we frequently make excuses or engage in self-pity. All too often we shut down or become prideful and defensive. So what about you? Stop and look over the list again. What are your top three most common anger responses?

Addictions are also often related to anger. People turn to drugs or alcohol to numb themselves or escape from their anger. Others turn to food for comfort when overcome with anger. Some of us seek distractions and busy ourselves with tasks or diversions in an effort to lessen anger's intensity. Workaholics, shopaholics, hedonists, and those with eating and substance-abuse disorders are often running from anger and its destructive power.

Anger Attitudes

Most of us don't want to admit we're angry, because we've grown up with the belief that *anger is bad* and should therefore be avoided or ignored at all costs. Unfortunately, those costs can be high. We expend tremendous time and emotional energy trying to control or deny (suppress or repress) our anger. Pretending anger doesn't exist or has been tamed when it hasn't can have devastating consequences.

Others believe that *anger is good and should be freely expressed.* In the last few decades, society encouraged the free and open expression of anger as a helpful way to unburden oneself. Unfortunately, freeing oneself from the negativity of anger has often become a higher priority than limiting the potential damage from venting it. "I have to get this out, to get this off my chest (even if it hurts you)." This conveys the idea that it's always best and emotionally healthy to express anger. It fails to acknowledge that there are times when it isn't in everyone's best interests to freely expose negative emotions.

Still others view anger as something they are *unable to change* or do anything about. They see it as genetically determined. "I can't control it. That's just the way I am." These people are generally referred to as hotheaded, short-fused, or quick-tempered, and they resign themselves to that label. They use their "I can't do anything about it" attitude as an excuse for not dealing with the problem. Meanwhile, people around them get wounded.

Psychological research and practice affirm the need to address anger. Counselors encourage the appropriate expression and monitoring of anger. It's considered a signal—a morally neutral, legitimate, God-given emotion. God's Word has provided effective answers on how to deal with it all along. *Anger is okay. It's what we do with it that counts.*

Factors That Affect How We Respond to Anger

How each of us responds to anger is affected by our personality, current circumstances, culture, gender, age, and past experiences. A thirty-year-old single, unemployed man from a divorced family will respond differently than a sixty-year-old disabled widower. A five-year-old African girl will respond differently than her counterpart in South America. A gregarious salesman will respond differently than a shy accountant. You get the point. Who we are, where we are, and what we have experienced all affect how we respond to anger.

Those with more expressive and vocal *personalities* are generally more likely to communicate or vent their anger. Introverts will most likely suppress their anger, keeping it inside. Our current *circumstances* affect how we respond, especially when we consider factors such as financial or relational stress, job satisfaction or unemployment, and marital and family status.

Some *cultures* embrace the assertive expression of anger, while others view anger as a problem to overcome. "Anger functions in any culture as a social regulator. It defines social behavior and protects societal values. Each culture determines when an angry response is appropriate and how that response is to be expressed. Anger is considered appropriate when the norms, mores, and laws of the culture are violated.

> **Who we are, where we are, and what we have experienced all affect how we respond to anger.**

This function of anger can be seen in the list of what makes people angry. The answers—rude people, prejudice, yelling, child abuse, and inconsiderate people—are all culturally determined. Each society sets the definition of rudeness, inconsideration, and child abuse."[2]

At an early *age*, children are allowed to cry, whine, and pout when angry, but the older they become, they are taught that these are inappropriate reactions. Though most of us haven't had courses in anger management, we are somehow supposed to know how to appropriately deal with it as we get older.

Gender can also affect how we respond. In most societies, it's generally more acceptable for a man to express anger than a woman. A man is viewed as assertive, a woman as aggressive; a man is considered strong, a woman pushy and unladylike. It is said that "ladies don't get angry." (For more on women and anger, see Harriet Lerner's best-selling book *The Dance of Anger*.[3])

Our *past experiences* also affect how we respond. Some have experienced abuse, gone through a divorce, lost a loved one, been betrayed, experienced prolonged illness, or had an unfaithful mate. Those from homes where anger was explosively displayed may either find themselves following the same pattern or doing just the opposite. Those raised in homes where any expression of anger was frowned upon most likely seek to control and contain it at all times.

The power of past experiences to shape our anger responses is widely recognized. Lorraine Bilodeau, author of *The Anger Workbook*, notes: "The frequency, intensity, and duration of painful anger episodes in your childhood determine the amount of power you bestow on anger, the level of fear you have about it, and the harshness with which you judge the person who is angry, yourself or another."[4] As you've probably observed, these early episodes can have long-lasting implications in your life.

When someone is mad at you, how do you respond? As a child, did you tell yourself that it was your fault—that you're stupid, bad, not good enough, going to show them, or going to get back at them? As adults, we generally respond with a grown-up version of our childhood responses: we try harder and work longer, we aim for perfection, we rebel and fight the system, or we try to be seen and not heard by withdrawing emotionally and sometimes even physically.

How have your circumstances, age, culture, gender, personality, family, and past affected your responses to anger? How was anger expressed or experienced in your family? How have you been shaped by your past? In what ways does your personality influence your emotional responses? It's amazing how much goes into shaping and forging this thing in us we call anger. If we're not careful, we can get terribly introspective at this point and feel so overwhelmed by the complexity of the issue that we experience paralysis rather than freedom. Try to resist getting bogged down in all the "whys" behind your anger—we've given them here as helpful background, not as an overwhelming checklist to address. Instead, let's get a basic grasp of the three major ways anger expresses itself in all of us.

Anger Profiles

We generally respond to anger in three distinct ways. We *spew it out* (exploding and expressing it), *stuff it* (hiding it and pretending it doesn't exist), or *leak it out* a little bit at a time. Though there are fancier names for each of these profiles, these will be easier to remember. They summarize them well and serve as memorable word pictures. We will refer to the three anger profiles as the Spewers, Stuffers, and Leakers.

Those who think they don't experience anger may learn that they have actually disguised or converted it into another emotion or action. Those who readily admit a problem with anger may better understand how they use it. The next three chapters explore these three kinds of responses. Read them thoroughly and thoughtfully. They describe all of us. You're likely to discover how and why you deal with anger the way you do.

The Bottom Line

Our circumstances, age, culture, gender, personality, family, and past all affect how we respond when angry. We've also developed attitudes about anger that can be detrimental to our ability to deal with it effectively.

Questions to Consider

1. How do you tend to react when you're angry? How many reactions from the list at the beginning of the chapter have you used?

2. How has your your current situation, your personality, your gender, age, and past affected how and when you get angry?

3. What is your anger attitude—your perspective on anger and the values you place on it? Is anger bad? Is it necessary? Should it always be expressed? Should it always be controlled or contained?

Action Steps to Take

- Ask a trusted friend or family member to help you identify your anger attitude. If that person is willing, also help him or her identify their own anger attitude.
- Take a few minutes to reflect on the possible problems that go along with each of these anger attitudes:

  Anger is bad.

  Anger should be openly and outwardly expressed.

  Anger responses (temperaments) can't change.

4

———

Spewers

It's easy to make fools of ourselves when angry.

It was a beautiful Saturday afternoon. I was working in the front yard, enjoying the sunshine and picking up the last of the yard clippings when my youngest son came running home.

"Dad, Dad, come quickly!" I ran up the street with him to find out what in the world might have gotten him so upset. As we came close to a nearby neighbor's door, I could hear screaming and yelling. Angry voices, name-calling, cussing, and the sound of crashing dinnerware grew louder and louder as we approached the house. My son's eyes were as big as saucers as he witnessed the trauma before us.

You see, the members of this family were new friends who had recently come to Christ after some very painful pasts. Their children and mine had become friends, and my boys were playing at their house at the time of this explosion. They had never seen anything like it and were scared to death.

For some of you, the above scene is commonplace—something you've witnessed hundreds of times. For others, it seems frightening and bizarre, especially in light of the fact that these were

THE MANY FACES OF ANGER

good people who genuinely loved one another. They both came from very dysfunctional and hurtful backgrounds and learned to express their anger by spewing it out on each other.

My wife Theresa would later meet with the wife, and I would meet with the husband as we sorted through all the pain and tried to help them learn to communicate in a way that focused on attacking the problems instead of each other. The fact is that we all learn to deal with our anger in ways that we've seen it growing up. In many families it's a very visible and sometimes frightening experience.

Spewers aggressively express their anger. They spew, spit, vomit, and explode their anger on those around them. They are forceful—like a time bomb waiting to go off or a volcano about to erupt. They yell, blame, and scream. They intimidate and control. They instill fear in those around them. Some even become physically abusive. They are often opinionated, forceful, blunt, tactless, demanding, and demonstrative.

A Spewer's motto is, "Yes, I'm angry. You bet I'm angry. I'm mad as #@%! and I have a right to say so!" To them the only way to get rid of anger is to get it out. They rarely take ownership of their emotions. They use statements like *"You* made me angry" instead of "I got angry when . . ."

Why Do We Blow Up?

Spewers fall into two distinct groups—out of control and in control. Those who are out of control are somewhat slaves to their anger. It has them on a leash, and they must go where it takes them. They let it all out because they don't know how to control or contain it. They feel helpless to tame it, so it runs wild. Afterward, they are filled with either remorse or rationalizations.

In-control Spewers are more deliberate and manipulative with their outbursts. They've learned that anger can be effective in controlling their environment and those around them.

They use it as a weapon of power and authority to accomplish their goals. They know what they are doing; their outbursts are often premeditated. Their anger is calculated and controlled, demanding and demeaning.

Are You a Spewer?

Most Spewers recognize themselves as such, though many aren't aware that their explosions are actually used as a means of control. If in doubt, see if these statements describe you. If you aren't sure, ask someone who knows you well. (And assure them it's okay to be honest!)

1. When I get mad I tend to let it out.
2. I don't hide my feelings when I'm mad; I let others know. I don't beat around the bush.
3. Sometimes I regret what I did or said in anger.
4. People who know me well might say that I have a quick temper.
5. My voice gets louder when I'm mad, and I'm more prone to cuss.
6. Others have said I can be intimidating when I'm mad.
7. Sometimes I feel out of control when I'm angry.
8. Sometimes I feel powerful when I'm angry.
9. When someone does something that makes me mad, I get defensive and want to retaliate.
10. Some might consider me opinionated.

You only need to agree with about half of the statements in order to identify yourself as a Spewer. If you do, you aren't alone. Don't assume that this problem is unique to you or that you are a horrible person. You can be a sincere Christian and still have problems with spewing. Rather than considering yourself hopelessly aggressive, simply realize that you have never learned to deal with anger constructively and begin that process now.

The story I shared at the beginning of this chapter was not of two terrible people. It was a story of two people who have learned to spew their anger. I cannot tell you how remorseful and repentant both were after the exchange, but much damage was done nonetheless. Many Spewers repeat this pattern over and over—explosions of anger followed by sincere remorse and apologies. If this sounds like you or someone you know, know that there's help and there's hope in the pages that follow.

The Costly Consequences

Those who aggressively express their anger also pay a high price for their outbursts.

The Emotional Cost

It's hard to verbalize how devastating angry outbursts can be to our souls. Often our explosions turn to inward contempt or rejection as we realize the damage done by our words. For some of us, our outward explosion is accompanied by an internal explosion of guilt, shame, embarrassment, and regret.

> It's hard to verbalize how devastating angry outbursts can be to our souls.

Others develop an even more self-righteous attitude, attempting to justify their behavior. "I had a right to do what I did. They did such and such to me." Rationalizing and justifying our raging tempers creates emotional monsters.

Those of us who use anger more as a controlled weapon develop a false sense of power. We use intimidation to control those around us, not realizing that our dominion gets smaller and smaller as people around us flee the relationship. Whereas we exercise power and feel powerful over others, we actually need to exercise more power (control) over ourselves.

The Relational Cost

The results of our explosions can be devastating, especially to those around us. When an angry coworker let loose on me several years ago, I felt I'd been riddled by her emotional rifle. She left feeling "so much better," having gotten the frustrations off her chest. I was left feeling wounded and bleeding all over. I started tiptoeing around that person and avoided her whenever possible.

We avoid Spewers like the plague. We walk on eggshells around them. We learn not to bring up certain topics. They become void of intimate relationships because they have alienated those around them.

There are bound to be casualties when we drop bombs on people. We lose friendships and strain relationships. People will keep their distance, and we may end up with few close friends who feel comfortable sharing their concerns or frustrations with us. The friends who remain are generally afraid to confront us for fear of retaliation or terrible consequences. As a result, our relationships become strained, lopsided, cautious, and very unhealthy.

> There are bound to be casualties when we drop bombs on people.

Another potential cost is retaliation from others. Our anger bombs may cause others to develop weaponry of their own. We may experience others' revenge as they attempt to pay us back for leaving them wounded.

The Physical Cost

During angry explosions, we tend to give ourselves permission to vent. We've either rationalized and justified our actions, or we've thrown our hands up in the air and said, "I can't help it. It's just the way I am." Whatever the reason, once we give ourselves permission to express anger, we are only a small step away from becoming physical. Here's a quote for exploders to remember, "Anger is just one letter short of danger."

We may hurt people or pets if we slap, kick, push, or hit. We may hurt things as we throw, break, or yank. You punch the door, you throw the book, you break the lamp. You shove, you slap, you kick, you beat. This kind of behavior is never acceptable or excusable. No human being, under any circumstance, deserves physical maltreatment. If you have stepped over the line, you need to get professional help immediately. Don't minimize it. Don't excuse it. Don't pretend it didn't happen. Go get help—*now!*

What Spewers Need

Those who spew need to learn to control their anger rather than using it to control others. They need to, as one writer says, "revoke permission" to express anger negatively. They need to stop denying and start acknowledging that their anger is destructive and detrimental. Exploders must learn to communicate anger in ways that don't destroy themselves or those around them.

But Spewers also need to know that change is possible. Expressing anger loudly or even violently is not an insurmountable behavior pattern. With the right help, the right understanding, and lots of prayer and support, Spewers can learn to express their anger appropriately without exploding. They can learn to share without shredding and to let the other person know without letting them have it—and to rebuild relationships that have been damaged by past outbursts. With God, redemption and restoration are always possible.

As Theresa and I worked with the couple in our neighborhood who had recently come to Christ but still experienced angry outbursts, one of the primary issues we dealt with was their false belief that they couldn't help themselves. Both were convinced that the only way to deal with angry feelings as they emerged was to spew them out. Both also learned to blame the other person and/or the circumstances for their angry spewing rather than own the problem personally. Although it takes great courage and some specific tools that we will be sharing throughout this book, I assure you I have seen many Spewers learn not only to get their anger under control but to actually use it as a means to facilitate their spiritual growth.

People who spew not only need to communicate anger effectively. They need, as we'll see in a few chapters, to communicate their needs. When we get in touch with our underlying hurts and needs, we are less likely to revert to quick, explosive encounters.

Summary: Spewers

Types: Exploding time bombs (out of control) and calculated time bombs (in control)

Message: Anger is necessary.

Reaction: "You bet I'm mad!" "Do what I say or else!"

Reasons for Expressing Anger
- ☐ It can give them a false sense of power or control.
- ☐ It helps them to release pent-up negative emotions.
- ☐ They feel unable to constrain or control anger (poor impulse control).

How They Blow Up
- ☐ Yelling, screaming, shouting
- ☐ Pushing, shoving, hitting, kicking
- ☐ Intimidation
- ☐ Aggression
- ☐ By becoming overly opinionated
- ☐ By being overly blunt, forceful, or tactless
- ☐ By being demanding and repetitive

Results
- ☐ They wound themselves and others
- ☐ Loss of control/power or a false sense of power
- ☐ Feelings of guilt
- ☐ Strained and unhealthy relationships
- ☐ Possible retaliation or revenge
- ☐ Possible damage from violent behavior
- ☐ Regrets

What Spewers (Exploders and Controllers) Need
- ☐ To develop a longer fuse
- ☐ To learn to control anger (deny themselves permission to be angry)
- ☐ To acknowledge their destructive expression and use of anger

☐ To learn to communicate anger effectively
☐ To learn to communicate needs effectively
☐ To learn what's "behind the anger" to use it constructively

The Bottom Line

Spewers are those who aggressively and forcefully express their anger. They spew, spit, vomit, and explode their anger on those around them. They are like a time bomb waiting to go off or a volcano ready to erupt. They use anger to intimidate and control but can improve their relationships dramatically by learning how to express their anger appropriately and constructively.

Questions to Consider

1. Are you a Spewer? If yes, do you feel out of control, or do you use your anger to control others?
2. Where did you learn to spew? Who gave you permission to express your anger like this?
3. How do you feel after you explode on someone?
4. What damage has your spewing caused in your relationships and your work?

Action Steps to Take

- Identify which items on the list of "What Spewers Need" are the highest priority for you.
- Share with someone you trust the areas on this list you want to work on, and plan together the practical ways in which you will be accountable to that person.
- If your spewing has resulted in physical abuse, seek professional help as soon as possible. You can receive forgiveness and God will help you change, but you must take the first step. Admit your need and ask for help.

5

Stuffers

Internalized anger often leads to internal combustion.

When Walter, a successful businessman, came in for counseling, it was "with pushing and prodding" from his family. He didn't think counseling could help but decided to give it a try. He shared about his business and how his partner was "taking over" in ways he didn't like. His family had repeatedly told him to talk to the partner, but he never did. When I (Becca) asked him why, he admitted, "I'm afraid of what I might say." He wanted to focus on what his partner did that angered him while I wanted to help him focus on ways he could deal with his anger more effectively.

When I first asked what his family was like growing up, he gave me a look that said, "What's this got to do with anything?" I pressed him on how his parents showed anger and what they did when they were angry. It became apparent as we talked that he had been taught to stifle anger. The unspoken but clearly understood family rule was "Don't get angry." Why? "Because it was un-Christian." He grew up being told that it was a sin. Since he tried to be a "God-fearing man," he had fought hard all his life to keep anger contained. But when his partner did some things that got deep under his skin, he found it hard to control his feelings.

Those who stuff their anger bottle it up inside. They don't want their anger to show, because they believe anger is bad. To show it would invite shame and disgrace. The goal for those who stuff is to keep a tight lid on anger. They avoid it at all costs because it's distasteful, deplorable, disgusting, and disgraceful.

The first step for Walter was to realize that it's okay to feel angry. It isn't a sin. As he began to accept it as a God-given gift, he was then open to learning constructive ways to deal with it.

Like Walter, you too might believe that anger is unacceptable and inappropriate. To display it is to display weakness. Many of us who stuff are Christians who incorrectly believe that it's a sin to show or have anger. We ignore it and pretend it's not there. If it shows its ugly face, we will attempt to bury it deep inside in hopes that no one, including ourselves, will see it.

It's All a Matter of Coping

Stuffers fall into two categories: those who *repress* or deny their anger and those who *suppress* or pretend anger doesn't exist.

Those who repress deny even having the feeling. They live in a fantasy world in which anger doesn't exist, at least not for them. They might admit to being a little "concerned," but that's all. The only anger acceptable to them is for the injustices of others—for the unborn, for child abuse and neglect, for hunger and starvation, for war crimes, for religious persecution, etc. Repressors have lost touch with their feelings. Many can no longer accurately recognize anger because they have denied it for so long.

Those who suppress their anger may know it exists, but they try to pretend it doesn't. They don't want to admit it or acknowledge it. *Their goal is to contain and control it.* They lean against the locked closet door of their emotions with all their strength to keep the beast from seeing the light of day. It's always dangerous; there are no angry kittens, only ferocious, roaring, hungry, man-eating anger lions.

Why We Stuff Our Anger

Because Stuffers falsely believe all anger is bad and sinful, they try to allow no room for it. Oftentimes the consequences of expressing it were so overwhelming when they were young that they decided not to feel anger ever again. Others may have been taught that anger was undignified—a sign of lack of control, to show it would be beneath them.

People pleasers often fall into this category. They will ignore their own feelings and risk losing touch with their own emotions in order to please others. Some may fear being rejected, losing another person's affection or attention. They see anger as a potential wedge in the relationship.

> **Because Stuffers falsely believe all anger is bad and sinful, they try to allow no room for it.**

Some who stuff their anger fear God's response. If "all anger is sinful," it invites God's wrath. Others don't like the guilt that accompanies feeling angry. Guilt is to be avoided, and anger brings guilt, so anger is also to be avoided. After a while, the person forgets how to feel anymore. These emotions don't simply die, however. They, like wandering spirits, come back to wreak havoc, haunting our emotional lives and relationships.

In some homes, the open expression or explosion of anger was scary. It was approached with fear and trepidation. Outbursts caused hurt and pain, both emotionally and perhaps physically. Growing up in that environment might have conditioned a person to see displays of anger as a quick way to make a fool of oneself. Their motto: "To lose one's cool is to be a fool."

59

This fear of retaliation and punishment may have been enough for some to stuff their anger for a lifetime. The consequences of showing it were too excessive, the cost too high, so they learned to ignore it.

Are You a Stuffer?

Does what we've described sound like you? Are you "cool, calm, and collected" even when chaos abounds and pressure mounts? Would friends say you get sullen, quiet, and withdrawn when they sense you are upset? If you want to know if the anger mask you wear is stuffing, read the following list. Then ask yourself, "Does this describe me?"

1. I don't feel comfortable with anger.
2. I tend to view anger as bad, something always to be avoided.
3. Growing up, anger was scary, and I feel very uncomfortable when others are mad.
4. Growing up, anger was never expressed in my family. The unspoken but well-understood rule was that anger was not okay.
5. I've seen too many people make fools of themselves in angry outbursts, and I swore I'd never do that.
6. I think I let others walk over me because I'm afraid to let them know when I'm upset.
7. Most people think of me as "cool, calm, and collected."
8. I'm uncomfortable sharing negative emotions with others.
9. I have some physical problems possibly related to stuffing my feelings.
10. I avoid confrontation!
11. I'm afraid of what will happen if I show anger (rejection, volcanic eruption, etc.).
12. God doesn't want us to get angry.

If you identified with several (about half) of these statements, you're probably a Stuffer. It doesn't mean you're bad. It doesn't mean you're a terrible person. It simply means that when anger knocks at the door, you stuff it down into your emotional hollow leg. We all deal with anger in ways we consciously and unconsciously learned since early childhood. The problem is that some ways are healthier than others. What you may not know is that stuffing can be harmful to your health.

The Costly Consequences

Those of us who stuff anger often do so at all costs—and the costs can be very high.

The Emotional Cost

Unexpressed anger often gets redirected at ourselves and can easily turn to inward resentment or self-hatred. It festers inside and doesn't go away. By burying it, we poison our own soul. When we clam up like tightly sealed shellfish, we're not oysters hiding prized pearls inside; we're clams with poisonous infections inside. We think we're terrible for feeling the way we do. This often leads to depression.

Avoiding anger causes us to shut down our emotions and lose touch with ourselves—with who we are and how we feel. We let others take advantage of us, because not showing anger is paramount, a higher priority even than standing up for ourselves. We'd rather become doormats than displease others. The emotional price tag is expensive.

The Relational Cost

In order to accomplish the mighty feat of keeping anger hidden, we become sullen, rigid, withdrawn, uptight, tense, easily aggravated, and controlling. This usually isn't a pleasant experience for those around us. We may find that we avoid certain people, places, and things that might trigger undesirable emotions in us. Our repressed anger becomes a gatekeeper at the door of our relational soul, forever excluding all who might awaken the sleeping giant within. Those who sense our inner anger may avoid us. They may detect an inner time bomb and not want to be around when it goes off.

Though Stuffers are good at stuffing, they may still erupt from time to time. Any relationships in the path of the volcanic flow can be deeply damaged.

The Physical Cost

Ned came to counseling to deal with the "overwhelming" stress in his life, which seemed to be the cause of his numerous physical ailments. He'd been to a chiropractor for tense back and neck muscles, to an internist for stomach pains, and to a neurologist for evaluation. He'd had X-rays, an MRI, numerous blood tests, a CAT scan, and several other tests. As our sessions progressed, it became clear to him that his physical concerns were not primarily the result of having too many pressures and demands in his life but of harboring intense resentments. As he began to admit his anger and to identify its root cause, his physical concerns began to lessen.

Many Stuffers pay a physical price—literally. Ulcers, headaches, back and neck pain, problems with indigestion, diarrhea, constipation, jitters, muscle tension, and high blood pressure are but some of the many manifestations of anger retention.

What Stuffers Need

Stuffers need to *accept anger* as a viable, allowable, normal, God-given emotion. They need to view anger as a helpful signal that notifies us that something is not right—either in us or in our situation. Anger is okay; it's what we do with it that counts.

They must also *acknowledge their fears and feelings.* Anger should be seen not as something to be afraid of but as something to be examined. They need to loosen fear's grip.

Stuffers must also *learn to communicate their needs effectively.* Having stuffed unwanted feelings for so long, they now need to be able to express them. They need to learn to be assertive with their needs and wants. Though they may fear seeming selfish, most who stuff anger err in the opposite direction—not standing up for their needs when needed. As they learn to communicate, they are better able to clarify what they will or won't do, how they really feel, and what they desire.

The Bottom Line

Those who stuff their anger bottle it up inside. They don't want their anger to show, because they believe anger is bad. To show anger is to invite shame and disgrace. The goal for those who stuff is to keep a tight lid on anger. Stuffers feel that anger is to be avoided at all costs because it is distasteful, deplorable, disgusting, and disgraceful. Stuffers are helped by accepting anger as normal, acknowledging their feelings, and learning to communicate effectively.

Questions to Consider

1. Are you a Stuffer? If so, have you bought into the belief that all anger is bad?
2. What can you do to help you stop stuffing your anger and pretending it's not there?
3. Which items on the list of "What Stuffers Need" do you most need to change?

Action Steps to Take

- Read over the list of "What Stuffers Need" (below). Share with someone you trust the areas you are asking God to change and then be accountable to that person.

- Consider buying an inexpensive spiral notebook and use it as a journal. I tend to stuff my anger, and privately writing out how I honestly feel has been very helpful.

- Begin asking yourself this question when you start feeling blue or depressed: "Could I be angry about something or at someone?" Then sit quietly for two or three minutes and let those feelings come to the surface.

Summary: Stuffers

Types: Repress (Deny/Avoid) or Suppress (Pretend/Stuff)

Message: Anger is bad.

Reaction: "Angry? Not me."

Why They Are Afraid of Anger
- ☐ They think it's bad, even sinful, to be angry.
- ☐ They fear God's wrath.
- ☐ They fear loss of control and making a fool of themselves.
- ☐ They fear rejection (others won't like them if they get angry).
- ☐ They don't like to feel guilty.
- ☐ Their experience with anger was scary, so all anger is something to be afraid of or avoided.
- ☐ They fear retaliation, punishment, the consequences or the possible outcomes of expressing anger.

How They Stuff Anger
- ☐ Ignoring it
- ☐ Denying it
- ☐ Shielding/deflecting it
- ☐ Minimizing it
- ☐ Pretending they aren't really angry
- ☐ Avoiding it
- ☐ Burying it

Results
- ☐ They become doormats (are taken advantage of).

- ☐ They redirect anger at themselves.
- ☐ They develop physical ailments: ulcers, muscle tension, headaches, etc.
- ☐ They occasionally erupt with volcanic-sized outbursts.
- ☐ They avoid people, places, and things.
- ☐ They develop resentments.

What Stuffers Need

- ☐ To accept that anger is okay/normal
- ☐ To acknowledge fears and seek to minimize their hold on others
- ☐ To learn to communicate anger effectively
- ☐ To become more assertive with their needs and wants
- ☐ To become clearer about what they will and won't do, and when

6

Leakers

Anger is still anger though it wears a disguise.

Bob couldn't understand what had gone wrong in his marriage. After five years of a healthy, happy relationship, he felt his wife drifting away and growing less affectionate all the time. He figured the demands of having two kids under the age of four explained her lack of interest in sex, but even when she seemed refreshed and they had times away together, she still made excuses or only participated halfheartedly.

What was wrong? Bob worked hard, was a good provider, and loved his wife and family. Sure, he watched too much football, and Cathy was always wanting him to "really open up" and get involved in the kids' lives. But these were normal issues in marriage, not major problems.

The truth was that whenever Cathy felt hurt or angry about some of Bob's tendencies, she expressed her feelings the way she had learned in her family: subtly, slowly, and passively. She was a Leaker, and Bob didn't have a clue.

The third profile is not quite as recognizable as the first two. In addition to the aggressors (Spewers) and the repressors and suppressors (two different kinds of Stuffers) we've talked about, there are also passive aggressors—those who let their anger leak out. Leakers tend to be critical, sarcastic, withdrawn, late, frigid, and "forgetful" in doing things for people who bug them, and procrastinate as a way of life.

As with Stuffers, Leakers don't like their anger to show. They may also come from homes where anger was either forbidden or excessively cruel and demeaning. They may have been taught that it's a sin that will invite the wrath of God. Whereas Stuffers pretend their anger doesn't exist, Leakers may agree to being angry—but just a little bit. They may acknowledge their anger but work hard at keeping it hidden.

Leakers are hesitant to express anger directly for the same fears and concerns Stuffers have. They believe that expressing anger brings a lot of pain, so they don't want to let others know they're mad. They think all confrontation leads to conflict, so they avoid sharing their true feelings. They essentially say to themselves, "I'm not going to stuff this anger inside, because that's not my style. And I'm not going to spew it out, because that's not my style, either. I'm going to do things that bother you and inconvenience you in order to make you hurt like I do. But I'm not going to let you know how I really feel. I'll just take it out on you in subtle ways." This is the attitude of the passive-aggressive.

How Do We Leak Our Anger?

We leak anger in two different ways: we either let it out in subversive, indirect ways by our behavior, or we let out little bits of verbal displeasure that we can disguise as "concern" or fact—but never to the person involved.

Some of us who are more verbal express our anger little bits at a time, thinking that it's more acceptable, appropriate, and proper that way. We'll gossip, make a negative comment here and there, and offer "constructive" criticism. All the while, our motive is revenge, whether we admit it or not. Instead of going to the person who offended us, we spread our anger around to everyone else. We slander, we disseminiate half-truths, we present information as if it were the gospel truth rather than our opinion, which is based on our hurt pride.

Unfortunately, I (Becca) know this profile all too well. I was fuming mad at a decision someone made, and instead of taking my disappointment and disagreement to the person in a mature, direct, loving manner, I began hunting for opportunities to make ever-so-brief derogatory, sarcastic comments. I knew that if I said too much, I would appear vindictive, so I calculated carefully when and where I would drop my seeds of dissension. Someone once said, "Not only is it difficult to say the right thing in the right place; it is far more difficult to leave unsaid the wrong thing at the tempting moment."[1]

> We'll gossip, make a negative comment here and there, and offer "constructive" criticism. All the while, our motive is revenge.

"Without wood, a fire goes out; without gossip, a quarrel dies down," we are told. It is often our gossiping that keeps the embers glowing when we need to let the fire go out. The apostle Paul, saddened by the Corinthians' behavior, wrote, "I fear that there may be quarreling, jealousy, outbursts of anger, factions, slander, gossip, arrogance and disorder [among you]" (2 Cor. 12:20).

Others of us are more active with our payback. We express our anger in our behavior by being continually late, procrastinating, and being unreliable. We withdraw when we know someone wants to talk to us. We commit to something with no intention of following through. We do things we know make others crazy. We will take a different pace just to annoy someone. When we get mad, we'll be late on purpose as a means of revenge. We will forget things at what seems to be the most inconvenient time possible, saying, "Oh, I didn't remember we agreed on that."

Leakers can be frigid, cold, unavailable, not feeling well, or confused. They are good at making excuses and at playing the helpless victim. They'll pout but say they aren't upset. Their "yeas" and "nays" aren't trustworthy. They are inwardly bitter and resentful, though others are often unaware of it. They often keep score internally. They've learned that their behavior is useful in enacting revenge. Deep inside, the goal of their anger is vengeance, and they pay you back in full. Though it's one of the more difficult masks to spot initially, once you understand it, you will begin to recognize it everywhere.

Are You a Leaker?

Do you let anger leak? Do you find subtle verbal and behavioral ways to get it out? Read over these statements to see if they describe you. Remember, you only need to agree with about half of the statements in order to determine if you leak out your anger.

1. I don't like dealing with people I'm angry with.
2. I try to hide my feelings when I'm angry.
3. When I'm mad at someone, I do things I know bother them.
4. I tend to hold grudges, not forgetting an offense easily.
5. I have engaged in gossip (sharing unkind thoughts about others).
6. I sometimes look for opportunities to indirectly get back at others.
7. When I don't want to do something, I pretend I don't know how to do it.

8. I'll go along with others (doing something I shouldn't) if I know it would adversely affect a person I'm mad at.
9. I don't like to admit when I'm angry.
10. I can be hard to pin down.
11. I talk about people behind their backs.
12. I can be critical and complaining.

As Christians we are commanded to deal with anger in ways that build others up rather than tear them down. Leaking our anger is unfair because our anger target hasn't been given the opportunity to explain, defend, or apologize. When I (Chip) leak my anger, I become an emotional coward, afraid to communicate negative feelings directly. Every anger-producing situation seems overwhelming to a Leaker, so we run and hide behind indirect verbal and behavioral darts. But there's hope. As we learn to identify our anger and its underlying cause, and as we develop tools to help us communicate our feelings, we can break out of this unhealthy pattern.

The Costly Consequences

Those who leak out their anger also pay a high price.

The Emotional Cost

Leakers run the danger of becoming bitter, spiteful, vengeful people. Their critical, negative attitudes easily take root and grow.

When we perceive that we've been wronged, we want to fight back. The Leaker fights back unfairly but feels empowered by his or her ability to get revenge indirectly. This false sense of power develops extremely harmful patterns of relating to others and of dealing with unwanted emotions.

The Relational Cost

When we don't deal with our anger in healthy ways, we jeopardize our relationships with a spouse, children, friends, family, or coworkers. Leakers tend to aggravate those around them. They say one thing and do another, which confuses and frustrates others. This puts a strain on relationships and weakens them.

> Leakers tend to aggravate those around them. They say one thing and do another, which confuses and frustrates others.

It doesn't take long for people to figure out where gossip, complaining, criticism, and slander came from. Gossip is like the goose that comes back and bites you in the bottom. As we alienate others we isolate ourselves. Over time, people will choose not to be around an unreliable whiner.

What Leakers Need

Like Stuffers, Leakers need to view anger as an acceptable emotion. They need to address the fears and beliefs that have kept them imprisoned. Rather than hide their anger, they need to bring it out into the open and deal with it. They must learn to communicate their anger effectively, clearly, and directly. They need to be assertive with their needs, wants, and desires. They also need to be clear about what they will and won't do and let their "yes" be "yes" and their "no" be "no." As they learn to do these things, they will be less afraid of letting anger show.

Questions to Consider

1. Are you a Leaker? If so, to what extent does the idea that expressing anger is bad resonate with you?
2. What is your most natural way of leaking—sarcasm, procrastination, verbal barbs, something else?

3. Who do you tend to leak out your anger on the most? Why do you think that person receives most of it?

4. Where did you learn to handle your anger in this way?

Action Steps to Take

- If you are a Leaker, read over the list of "What Leakers Need" (below). Share with someone you trust the areas you are asking God to change, and then be accountable to that person.

- Identify at least one person close to you toward whom you have "leaked" your anger, and then acknowledge to that person that you are aware of your tendency and are working on it.

- Ask God to show you any grudges or bitterness you may have held on to. Whenever a past offense comes to mind, pray a prayer of forgiveness and ask God to release you from the anger it caused.

Summary: Leakers

Types: Indirect and Direct

Message: Showing anger is bad.

Reaction: "Angry? Not me. Well, maybe just a little."

Why They Are Afraid of Anger
- ☐ They think it's bad, even sinful, to be angry.
- ☐ They fear God's wrath.
- ☐ They fear loss of control, losing it, making a fool of themselves.
- ☐ They fear rejection (others won't like them if they get angry).
- ☐ They don't like to feel guilty.
- ☐ Their experience with anger was scary, so all anger is something to be afraid of or avoided.
- ☐ They fear retaliation, punishment, or the consequences or possible outcomes of expressing anger.

How They Leak Anger
- ☐ By not following through on commitments or promises
- ☐ By not letting their "yea" be "yea" and their "nay" be "nay"

☐ By making excuses
☐ By procrastinating
☐ By knowingly going at a pace different than and annoying to others
☐ By playing possum (or the helpless, ignorant victim role)

Results

☐ They develop a false or unhealthy sense of power.
☐ They aggravate those around them and strain/weaken relationships.
☐ They become critical and negative.
☐ They become isolated.

What Leakers Need

☐ To accept that anger is okay/normal
☐ To acknowledge fears and seek to minimize their influence
☐ To learn to communicate anger effectively
☐ To become more assertive with their needs and wants
☐ To become clearer about what they will and won't do, and when

Which Is Worse?

As you can see, we tend to respond to anger differently, depending on who we are. We've seen that even though we may not be a screamer who blows up all the time, we may still have a problem with anger. Just because we stuff it and keep it in doesn't mean we're dealing with it correctly. Many mistakenly believe that the only negative profile is the explosive type. But as we've seen, stuffing and leaking are equally harmful.

What's Your Anger Profile?

With which of the profiles do you most identify? What anger related issues do you need to address? We all have anger issues, regardless of personality or spiritual maturity. In the next chapter, we will begin the exciting journey of seeing how to use our anger to better understand ourselves, relate to others in healthy ways, and grow in our intimacy with God. Why not read over, once again, what your anger mask needs and get started on it? Later chapters provide some practical help, but you may also find professional help to be necessary or beneficial. Don't procrastinate. Don't say, "You can't teach an old dog new tricks. I can't change." Don't give up; get help. With God's grace, you can do it.

These last several chapters helped identify your anger profile and what you might need to change. The next chapter, however, is pivotal to your understanding of anger. If you were to read only a few chapters in this whole book, this should be one of them. If you really want to get ahold of anger, if you want to overcome the destructive components that accompany it, understanding the next point will put you well on your way.

PART 3

WHY WE ALL STRUGGLE WITH ANGER

7

Anger Is a
Secondary Emotion

One of the first things for which we have to pray is a true insight into our condition.

—Olive Wyon

After a long workday of early morning meetings, several "crises," and an evening meeting, I (Chip) was looking forward to getting home to be with my wife, Theresa. She's my best friend, my counselor. I really wanted to talk with her, to feel connected, to find out about her feelings and her day, and to share with her some things going around in my head. I wanted to bounce some ideas off her, get her thoughts, find out how the kids were doing, and just be together. Perhaps we'd have a cup of tea or coffee and enjoy a good conversation. She'd give me a big hug and say, "It's okay. God's big, and I love you," and all that other stuff I want to hear. I was also thinking that I hadn't been able to spend much time with my son, Ryan, and he's always fun. And my little girl, Annie, would be excited about reading some new books. I hoped to get home in time to hear about some of them.

I got home around 9:15 p.m., and the house was already dark. Very dark. Everyone was in bed. I tiptoed into the bedroom, thinking Theresa was probably just lying there in the dark waiting for me so we could have a good talk. But she wasn't waiting for anything; she was sound asleep. I went to Plan B and headed for Ryan's room, but he was out too. And by this time, Annie had long been asleep. I felt hurt. Lonely. Sad. I didn't get to process things. I needed someone to be there for me, but no one was. My head told me I was wrong to expect them to stay awake all the time waiting for me. After all, they didn't know I really needed them that evening. But my heart ached. I was hurt.

So what did I do? I got mad. Mad at my family for not being there for me. Mad at my crazy week. Just mad. I went to bed and took my anger with me. And I've found over the years that when I go to bed with a little anger, if I haven't resolved it before I sleep, it grows.

When I got up the next morning, I still had that edge. But I wasn't aware of it. I didn't make the connection between my hurt feelings turning to anger the night before and my bad mood the next morning. I got dressed, walked out into the hall, saw my daughter. "Annie," I said sharply, "go make your bed!"

"But, honey, she just got up," Theresa said.

"I don't care if she got up or not. Make your bed! And Ryan, have you done your chores yet, have you had your quiet time?"

"Dad, I just . . . ," Ryan stammered.

"Honey!"

Then I wrapped it up: "Hey, if the morning is going to be like this, forget it. I'm going to the office. I've got a lot to do."

I went out, got in the car, and shut the door. *No one appreciates me*, I thought. *No one is there for me.* After fuming for several minutes, I finally admitted to myself that I was angry. Then I remembered what I've been saying about anger being a secondary emotion and asked myself, "What's going on? Why am I feeling so angry?" I realized I was really feeling hurt, lonely, and disappointed.

The Holy Spirit prompted me with that still small voice: "Well, what are you going to do about it, Chip? Are you going to just drive away and not deal with it?" Finally, after at least ten minutes, I got out of the car and went inside. "Honey, I'm sorry I blew up at you this morning. I was feeling lonely, and I needed you." I explained how I'd felt beat-up yesterday and what my needs, hurts, and expectations were. She turned to me, put her arms around me, looked me in the eye, and said, "Well, honey, maybe we could make time to talk today." *What a novel idea!* I thought.

Then I went to my son. "Ryan, I'm sorry I blew up at you. It wasn't you. It's just that I missed you so much last night that when you weren't awake, I decided to take it out on you by yelling at you this morning. And so I'm sorry." When I saw my daughter, I said, "Annie, honey, you didn't do anything wrong. You just happened to be in the hall at the wrong time." And I went on to explain it as well as I could to a child. Although this event happened nearly ten years ago, I remember it as if it took place yesterday. It was one of the first times I ever connected my anger to the deeper, unresolved issues in my heart.

It's Easier to Be Angry Than to Face the Deeper Issues

It's vitally important to understand anger is the outside emotion sent to protect the inner, more sensitive aspects of our hearts. It's a secondary response that hides a deeper or more sensitive issue. If we grasp this point, we'll be well on our way to dealing with anger in constructive ways. When we feel angry, we need to ask ourselves, "*Why* am I feeling this way?" Anger isn't the first feeling to come, though it's generally the first one to show outwardly. Wherever it surfaces, another emotion already existed.

When I (Becca) was very late to pick up my son from school, I got mad at the clock, the school, the traffic lights, my watch, and the school's schedule before I finally admitted the real issue: that I was embarrassed that the school secretary had to call me. When a client of mine got mad at his boss, he realized that the strong underlying emotions were really insecurity and fear, not anger. When I got mad at a driver who made a visual gesture at me, I later realized that the root feeling was guilt because I had pulled out too far and was dangerously blocking traffic. When I got angry at a colleague for not including me on a decision, I discovered hurt pride underneath. If you and I are honest with ourselves and brave enough to peel back the anger, we can discover its true motivating force.

When people abandon us, when they let us down, when someone doesn't come through, when we feel rejected, left out, lonely, sad, or sorrowful, we generally cover it up with anger. Because these emotions are so strong, painful, and confusing, anger serves as a more satisfying substitute. What did Cain do? Did he face feeling sad, rejected, and jealous? No. Instead, he acted on his anger and killed his brother Abel. Anger artificially helps us feel in control when we're feeling out-of-control and falsely helps us feel powerful when we feel powerless.

Anger Is Not the Problem; It's the Warning Light

Anger is like the red warning light that comes on the dashboard of your car. Our error is that we tend to view the problem as the light rather than what it's indicating. Even if we take the dashboard apart and replace the bulb, the problem is still there.

It's still red! Why? There's something wrong with the car, not with the light.

Anger is not the problem

This secondary emotion tells you something is wrong under the *emotional* hood, under the *spiritual* hood, or under the *relational* hood of your life. Most of us spend too much time trying to figure out how we can get rid of our anger when we should be asking ourselves, "What's going on inside that's making me angry?" To resolve your anger, you'll need to identify the root reason for it.

> To resolve your anger, you'll need to identify the root reason for it.

Anger is a secondary response telling us that something is missing, wrong, or uncomfortable and needs to be checked, fixed, or changed

Anger is a tool of communication. We use it to express our hurt or frustration and to protect and preserve. It communicates beyond the spoken word and through its intensity. Our job is to decipher what it's really trying to say.

One day when my oldest daughter was about seven years old, I (Becca) asked her to do something that normally would have been met with, "Okay, Mom." This time, however, the response was, "I don't want to. Why do *I* have to do it?" When I repeated the request, not quite so kindly this time, she lost it and screamed, "No, I won't do it! You're such a mean mom!"

At that point my anger was beginning to flare, as if she'd blown a mighty breath onto glowing embers. I was about ready to yell back with the fury of an authoritative, power-driven parent when I stopped for a moment and thought about her day. She'd had a very long, busy, physically exhausting day for a second grader (school, spelling test, Girl Scout meeting, and soccer practice). After a day full of demands and activities, she needed a break. It wasn't so much that she was mad at me but that she was tired. As I was able to look beneath her angry outburst, I saw what really fueled her statements. She didn't have the skills to say, "Gee, Mom, I'm really exhausted right now. I've had a very long, tiring day. Could you get someone else to do it, or could I just do it later?" At seven, it's hard to sort out and communicate what you're really feeling. In fact, it's hard to sort out and to communicate what we're really feeling at any age!

What's the Root Reason?

When was the last time you got angry at someone or something? If anger is a secondary emotion, then what fueled it for you? Was it hurt, loneliness, and disappointment like Chip? Embarrassment, guilt, or pride like Becca? Exhaustion (stress) like Becca's daughter? Insecurity and fear like the employee? There are many emotions we might find under the hood if we were to take a closer look. Here's a list of some of the feelings that often fuel anger. Which ones most commonly fuel yours?

- hurt
- guilt
- shame
- powerlessness
- betrayal
- insecurity
- rejection
- dashed hopes and dreams
- feeling trapped
- hopelessness
- helplessness
- unmet expectations

- resentment
- envy, jealousy
- pride
- low self-esteem
- failure
- sense of worthlessness
- loneliness
- depression
- worry, anxiety
- pressured, stressed out
- disappointment
- remorse
- exhaustion, fatigue
- grief

When we're jealous, we get mad. When we're embarrassed, we get mad. When we feel guilty, we get mad. When we feel resentment, grief, depression, pride, helplessness, betrayal, rejection . . . we get mad. For most people—some Stuffers not included, perhaps—anger is easy to identify. It's uncovering and identifying what caused the anger that's tricky.

The Needs behind the Anger

The list of underlying emotions could go on and on. We believe, however, that many of them can be grouped into three categories. We will discuss these in more detail and provide some theological insight and practical suggestions to help in the coming chapters, but for now here's a quick overview.

First, anger may indicate that we have unmet needs and are feeling hurt. As human beings, we have a variety of needs. We need to belong; to have relationships; to be connected, loved, supported, and encouraged; and to feel worthy, capable, and competent; and we need autonomy, space, independence, and freedom of expression. When these needs aren't met, we feel hurt. And when we feel hurt, we generally get angry. We may direct it externally at people, places, and things, or we may turn it inward, which leads to low self-esteem and depression. Like Chip with his family, anger often reveals our inner hurt, which can include fear, sadness, loneliness, disappointment, rejection, worry, a sense of loss, and much more.

Unmet expectations are the second area in which anger manifests itself and leads to feelings of frustration. When things don't go the way we want, we get frustrated. When plans change unexpectedly, when goals are blocked, when dreams are dashed and hopes are abandoned, anger is fast on their heels. Our expectations set us up for disappointment when they are unrealistic or inapplicable to the person or situation. Becca's rising anger was fueled by an unrealistic expectation that her daughter would obey and respect her at all times. When we feel frustrated, we may feel annoyed, trapped, scared, embarrassed, resentful, or unhappy, among others.

When we feel threatened, anger may also be covering up feelings of insecurity. Whether the threat is real or perceived, emotional or physical, we respond with anger because it helps protect or shield us. What is really going on when someone cuts you off or puts you down, ignores your input, or passes you over? When our self-esteem is under attack or our well-being in danger, we feel insecure. When we feel insecure, we may feel ashamed, nervous, inadequate, humiliated, prideful, or terrified. And when we feel insecure on the inside, we let anger show on the outside.

To summarize, when people don't come through for us, when we think God has let us down, when we feel hurt or wounded, it means we didn't get a need or an expectation met. That can cause us to feel weak, hurt, and vulnerable. If someone threatens us, those we love, our job or lifestyle, or anything else important to us, we feel insecure. When this happens, we often rely on anger to protect and preserve us. It isn't the problem. It's the warning light that there is a problem—a problem that needs our attention.

> **It's the light on the dashboard that signals that something is wrong under the hood.**

The Bottom Line

Anger is a secondary emotion that hides deeper issues. It's the light on the dashboard that signals that something is wrong under the hood. It's the way we protect ourselves from hurt, frustration, and insecurity. It has positive potential, but if it goes unchecked, it also has negative ramifications. Here's a summary of the three categories of primary emotions.

Three Main Anger Zones

Hurt from unmet needs	*Frustration* from unmet expectations	*Insecurity* from threatened self or self-esteem

Questions to Consider

1. What are the most common sources of anger in your life (e.g., the kids, the bills, your neighbor, the company, your spouse, traffic)?
2. Why is it so important to realize that anger is a secondary emotion?
3. Taking off the anger mask and exposing what's underneath can be a painful and/or liberating process. Which of the three root causes underlying our anger (hurt, frustration, insecurity) do you most easily identify?

Action Steps to Take

- Look over the long list of primary emotions again and put a check mark next to the four or five most common reasons for your anger.
- The insight that anger is a secondary emotion may help you understand not only yourself but also others around you. Share that insight with someone in your circle of family and friends who needs to understand it.
- Try to remember at least two or three times you were really angry. Then ask yourself, "What was the emotion hidden under the anger?"

8

The Tip of the Iceberg

If anger is only the tip of the iceberg, our challenge is
to look into the icy waters below.

Not long ago, I (Becca) visited the beautiful cities of Sitka and Juneau in southeast Alaska. I went on a daylong boat trip up the Tracy Arm Fjords to view wildlife and glaciers. Massive rock walls, carved long ago by advancing glaciers, towered above each side of the large tourist boat. As we neared the final destination, the Sawyer Glacier, we began seeing icebergs floating in the frigid water. I especially remember one large iceberg floating in front of a cascading waterfall. This particular iceberg was about twenty-five feet tall—about the height of our boat. It was a breathtaking and beautiful sight. Then the captain reminded us that we were seeing only a small part of the entire iceberg; only about 14 percent shows above the water while most lies deep beneath the surface. I tried to calculate the possible depth of that mass of ice and realized that a twenty-story structure extended down into the water beside us!

Anger is like the tip of the iceberg. It's often what shows, but it isn't really indicative of the whole problem. Down below are the primary emotions that push anger to the surface. As we learned in chapter 7, anger is just a secondary signal letting us know there's something wrong underneath.

Let's identify the ways anger surfaces. If you remember from past chapters, we tend to spew, stuff, or leak our anger. But underneath, hidden below the surface, lie the primary reasons: unmet needs (hurt), unmet expectations (frustration), and threatened self (insecurity). This is where you'll want to direct most of your effort. Why work on superficial issues when you can get at the root? This is the level that can change how you deal with anger.

If you're going to grow, you'll need to ask yourself if there's an unmet need in your life. Is there loneliness or sadness? Is there a blocked goal? Are you feeling threatened or insecure? Are there unresolved issues that are hard to face?

God wants to get at what's below the surface and bring about supernatural healing. Instead of being enslaved by anger, anger can become your slave. It can tell you things that are going on in your heart that you've never known before.

We Need to Weed

Forcing yourself to face the root causes of anger might be harder than you think. For some of us, the difficulty is that the root

emotion is buried beneath layer after layer of anger or denial. For others, the emotion may be near the surface but too painful to face. To look at something you may have avoided, hidden, or buried for so long won't be easy.

When I (Chip) was a kid growing up, I cut eight or ten lawns a week. I generally enjoyed it, but one of the jobs I didn't like was being asked to weed. I learned very quickly that you could just use clippers to clip off the top and be done fast. The problem, of course, was that the next week, the weeds would be there again.

> Anger is like the tip of the iceberg. It's often what shows, but it isn't really indicative of the whole problem.

I soon learned that the best way to get weeds out is to pour a little water on the soil to get the ground soft. Then it's easier to dig down and get the whole weed—root and all. But to do this, I had to get my fingernails dirty. Once I got the whole weed out, however, I didn't have to deal with it again.

This is what many of us do with anger. Instead of dealing with the root reason feeding the anger, we shortcut the process and look only at ways to control our temper. The deeper issues will resurface again and again and again. To get rid of anger's destructive hold on us, we too must dig down deep and do some dirty work.

Looking Below Takes Courage

Looking below not only takes dirty work; it takes courage. Many of us would just as soon stay on the surface and deal with anger. It's familiar and already exposed. We don't want our deeper hurts, frustrations, and insecurities to show. But when the dashboard warning light goes on, we mustn't try to fix the light or change the bulb. We need to look under the hood. We must have the courage to look at what is really going on.

Facing issues we've run away from or hidden can be scary, but it's the first step on our journey. If you need encouragement or support, get it. Don't be afraid to ask someone for help. I (Chip) had a hard time admitting that I had an anger problem, let alone asking for help. But when the conflict and lack of communication in my marriage forced me to face my Leaker tendencies, Theresa and I went to a Christian marriage counselor who helped us identify our anger and then provided some practical tools to help us express and deal with our anger positively. Was it hard? Yes! Life changing and liberating? Absolutely! We very often work so hard at covering up the real reasons for our anger that some of us have either forgotten there's anything underneath or have forgotten how to feel. You'll be better off if you deal with the deeper issues. Yes, that may be hard, but in the infamous words

> Facing issues we've run away from or hidden can be scary, but it's the first step on our journey.

of Dr. Phil when counseling people stuck in negative patterns, "How's that working for you?" Not facing the primary emotions can leave you a prisoner to anger forever.

So let's take a look at a simple and practical way for you to move from the "anger light" on your dashboard to looking under the hood and discovering the real issue.

The Anger ABCDs

Our goal, then, is to acknowledge our anger and find out what's beneath it. If we're successful at this task, we'll be on our way to freeing ourselves. From our own personal experience as well as from the personal testimony of many people who have done it, we believe *the Anger ABCDs can transform lives.*

The Anger ABCDs help us deal with the issues in a simple, basic, and easy-to-follow way. This will be presented in more detail in a later chapter, but for now, here's what you need to get started.

A **Acknowledge** that you're angry.
Don't deny it or stuff it; admit, accept, and acknowledge it.

B **Backtrack** to the primary emotion.
Ask yourself: Why am I angry? What am I *really* feeling? What is the root reason for my anger?

C **Consider** the cause.
Ask yourself: Who or what caused it to occur? Who or what frustrated me? Who hurt or wounded me? What plans fell through? *What happened?*

D **Determine** how best to deal with it.
Ask yourself: How should I respond? What should I do? When? How?

Even though some of your anger may be directed at God, we encourage you to take your hurt, frustrations, and insecurities to him. He won't let you down. He's the one person who can meet your every need, who can give you realistic expectations, and who can be your source of security. He can help walk you through this journey of dealing with this emotion that can destroy you, uncovering the vulnerabilities and pain underneath.

The Bottom Line

We believe anger is one of the most pressing issues we can study that will transform the way we relate to one another. Anger lets us know that something is wrong. Our job is to figure out the real issue underneath it. We pray that God gives you the courage to face your anger, as this can begin a revolutionary process of changing you from the inside out.

> **Anger lets us know that something is wrong. Our job is to figure out the real issue underneath it.**

You will get better and better with the ABCDs of anger as you practice. Don't be anxious or uptight if you struggled to answer some of the above questions. The real first step is simply learning to start asking these questions when you're angry. In the next three chapters, we're going to deal with the three underlying issues of our anger. You'll learn to see yourself and your needs and learn how to deal with the hurt, unmet needs, and insecurities that are common to us all.

Questions to Consider

1. How difficult is it for you to openly share your feelings?
2. How does the iceberg illustration help you understand your anger and its accompanying emotions?

3. How do you think your life would change if you began to see anger as a "friend" who wanted to let you know "something's wrong under the hood" to prevent you from wrecking a relationship?

Actions Steps to Take

- Think of two times recently when you were really angry at someone or something. Now go through the ABCDs to identify what you were really feeling and why.

The Anger ABCDs

A **Acknowledge** you are/were angry.
Admit and accept your anger.
"I was angry at _____ when he/she _____."

B **Backtrack** and identify the primary emotion(s).
Ask yourself what you were really feeling.
"What I really felt was _____ (hurt, frustrated, wounded, etc.)."

C **Consider** the cause. (What contributed to the feelings?)
Ask yourself what happened and why you felt that way.
"I felt this way because _____."

D **Determine** how to deal with it.
How did you respond to this situation?
What would it look like to address this anger issue in a positive way?
- Talk with God about how you felt and why?
- Evaluate your response and apologize if necessary?
- Recognize that you were rightfully angry and that this good anger should motivate you to some positive response?

- How did you deal with the situations you identified? Read over the "D" section in the above chart and put it into practice this week.

9

Hurt from Unmet Needs

No man is angry who feels not himself hurt.

—Francis Bacon

After hearing Chip speak and realizing that anger is a secondary emotion, a woman wrote a note in which she shared how she had been feeling very hurt and depressed. She had been deeply involved helping a friend through a painful part of her life. God used this woman mightily to help her friend. As the friend became more and more emotionally healthy and independent, God brought a "wonderful" mate into her life. The helper had prayed for the person's healing and happiness, but when it came, she found herself feeling angry. As she looked below the anger, she discovered sadness, loneliness, and hurt. "Everything has been put in perspective for me now," she concluded. She had liked being needed and important, and now she didn't seem needed anymore. And now she saw the whole picture. She faced her anger and found what lay underneath. Instead of cutting off the top of the weeds, she learned to dig deep and get at the root reason for her anger—hurt. Dealing with the true source helped her anger subside.

This first step in overcoming anger's destructive side is recognizing it's not the problem. It's a surface symptom telling us there's an infection inside. Are you beginning to realize the importance of seeing it as secondary? Have you stuffed, spewed, or spilled your anger because down deep you're hurt, frustrated, and wounded? In chapter 8 we briefly shared what we consider to be the three root reasons for anger: hurt (unmet needs), frustration (unmet expectations), and insecurity (threatened esteem). We'll examine each of these in the next few chapters, along with a practical tool to help.

> This first step in overcoming anger's destructive side is recognizing it's not the problem. It's a surface symptom telling us there's an infection inside.

Joseph's Brothers

Do you remember the story of Joseph and his brothers?[1] Their father showed partiality to Joseph, the youngest, giving him preferential treatment and a special multicolored coat. His brothers got mad—they were furious. Why? Because their dad let them down. They felt unloved, unspecial, and unimportant—rejected, jealous, and sad. They felt hurt.

But it takes courage to be vulnerable and tell others when we're hurting. For these brothers, it was hard to say that their dad let them down. So what did they do? They resorted to anger because it made them feel strong instead of weak and powerless. They planned to kill Joseph but ended up selling him as a slave. We all have the potential to do terrible deeds when motivated by anger.

When we're angry, we should start by asking ourselves, "Am I hurting?" Once we discover hurt, we need to get more specific: "What's the hurt about?" Are we hurting because we feel

> **When we're angry, we should start by asking ourselves, "Am I hurting?"**

guilty, jealous, rejected, lonely, betrayed, unappreciated, unloved, or ashamed? It's important to identify our unmet needs and hurt feelings so that we can more effectively seek to heal and deal with them.

Communicating the Hurt

Throughout the book of Psalms in the Old Testament, we find David lamenting, "Hey God, what's the deal? How come the wicked are prospering and I'm getting a raw deal? I don't understand it, and I'm really upset. You anointed me king, but now I'm catching spears from this guy named Saul. And God, if you've got this great plan for my life, how come I'm running around with this band of hobos, sleeping in caves at night, and running for my life? Hey God, my count is down, I'm ticked off. How long are you going to ignore my situation? How long are you going to let this go on? Where are you? What are you doing? This is unfair, God! Do you even care?"

About one fourth of the Psalms are referred to as the "lament psalms" in which a godly man expresses his disappointment and hurt. Where does he go to express it? To God. *It's okay to express our hurts to God. He understands.*

But did you know that most of those psalms end with a recognition of God's love and greatness? Though they start with pain, they usually end with praise. "O God," he says, "who could I turn to but you. You are my healer, my shield, my rock, and my redeemer. I was just blowing off steam. I was just hurting. I've just been let down. Who else could I go to? I will praise you, Lord, for you are a great, loving, and merciful God. Even though I don't understand, I will still trust you."

We need to make some of our own lamenting psalms. We need to take our hurt to God. We need to make our needs known.

As I (Chip) learned to recognize and deal with the same deeper issues behind my anger, I realized I needed some tools to help me. It didn't come naturally to ask the kind of questions we are recommending, so I started by keeping a journal. It wasn't anything fancy—just writing out thoughts and feelings and processing issues in my heart in a safe place.

In the following pages, we want to give you some tools to help you begin to move beyond the anger and deepen the relationships that matter most.

Tool #1: Communicate Needs

Making our needs known requires two things:

- we need to be able to identify what they are, and
- we need to be able to communicate them effectively.

So far we've been talking about the first part. We've learned that we have to stop and ask ourselves what we're feeling and why. Now let's work on how we communicate our needs to others in ways that are nonthreatening and clear.

Counselors have been teaching this tool for years, and people say that they have found it to be both helpful and easy to remember. Once we identify the primary emotion (the root reason for our anger), we simply say what we call an "I feel" statement. "I feel _____ (the primary emotion) when _____ (what happened)." It's two simple steps:

1. "I feel _____
2. when _____."

When we use "I feel _____ when _____" statements, this "presents two pieces of information about yourself. It tells the

97

other person your interpretation of his behavior and your feeling reaction to that interpretation. It also provides the opportunity for him to let you know whether your interpretation is
accurate."[2]

Early on in our marriage, Theresa and I were knocking heads
a bit. Psychologically and emotionally, she was born somewhere
near the North Pole, and I was born near the South Pole. We
were both totally committed to God and to each other but were
experiencing some frustrating times. In talking to one of my
seminary professors, we came to realize that we didn't express
our anger appropriately. We both knew that screaming and
throwing things at each other was not the Christian response.
(Christians learn more sophisticated ways to deal with their
anger.) I was passive-aggressive (a Leaker). Whenever I was
mad at Theresa, I would be late—my way of paying her back.
Whenever Theresa was mad at me, she'd withdraw and get quiet
(a Stuffer).

We came to admit we had immature ways of dealing with
anger. We were taught in marriage counseling about "I feel . . ."
statements and put this tool on a 3 × 5 card on our refrigerator,
where it stayed for two years. I'll never forget the first night
Theresa used it on me. I came home late on a night she had
planned a romantic candlelight dinner for just the two of us.
I was in the car thinking of my defense, of all of my possible
excuses (which usually involved some exaggeration—and lack
of integrity). But I had my offense planned as well. I had discovered that when I attacked her first, things usually went a
little better. I entered the house both offensively and defensively
ready, expecting her to nag or yell or shut down. But after kindly
greeting me at the door and serving me dinner, complete with
candles, she calmly looked me in the eyes and said, "Chip, I feel
very hurt and unloved when I work hard to express my love to
you and you show up thirty to forty-five minutes late." I was

stunned. I wished she had just gone ahead and nagged me—I could fight nagging. I wanted to say, "Get up and fight like you're supposed to. Nag, yell, fight, do something." But she didn't explode. She didn't stuff it. She didn't withdraw. She loved me and she leveled me. She shared honestly and under control, *"I feel hurt when . . ."* After about two years, that became a pattern of communication in our lives.

Communicating our feelings in this way takes maturity and requires ownership of our feelings. We no longer say, *"You* made me feel _____ when *you* did _____." We take responsibility for our feelings using "I" statements instead of "you" accusations. "I feel hurt when you come home late." "I feel hurt when you spend money outside the budget." "I feel hurt when you aren't very affectionate." "I feel hurt when you give your time to work and other people and there's little left for me." "I feel _____ when _____." Put it on a 3 × 5 card, carry it with you, put it on your refrigerator—wherever works best. But be sure to use it.

This kind of response brings understanding and prevents anger from escalating. It deals with your feelings and the issues instead of attacking the person. It isn't hard to learn, and with a little practice, it will revolutionize your communication. Unresolved anger in marriage kills intimacy, friendship, and sexual attraction. Put the "I feel" message on a 3 × 5 card and start with some low-risk statements today.

Using "I Feel . . ." with the Anger ABCDs

We can incorporate the "I feel . . ." statements into the first three Anger ABCDs:

A Acknowledge you are/were angry.
B Backtrack and identify the primary emotion(s) or root reasons for the anger.
Ask yourself, "What am I really feeling?", then say, *"I feel . . ."*

C Consider the cause

Ask yourself, "What happened? Why am I feeling this way?" then say, *"When . . ."*

"I feel" messages are healthy because there's no attack. It's an honest expression of how you feel. It opens up the door for dialogue and increased maturity. Anger can then become the signal to which you respond, "Here's an opportunity to communicate and to grow." If you use this, it can impact your life greatly.

Someone Who Understands Our Hurt

When you're hurting and your needs aren't being met, there's someone who understands and will be there for you—no matter what. God is the only one who will come through 100 percent of the time, and he's demonstrated that through Christ's work on the cross and his love and compassion. He's the only one who can meet the deepest longings of your heart. People will let you down, but he never will. He says, "I will never leave you nor forsake you."

The Bottom Line

It's absolutely critical to identify our unmet needs and hurt feelings so that we can more effectively deal with them. We need to learn to openly and clearly communicate our feelings rather than run to anger to protect or insulate us. Will this happen overnight? No. But with practice, it can put out the anger fires of ongoing conflict and eliminate the smoldering coals of bitterness and resentment.

Questions to Consider

1. How effective do you think "I feel. . ." statements would be in your life? Are you skeptical? Unwilling? Apprehensive? Why?

2. Who is a safe friend with whom you could share what you learned in this chapter?
3. What risks would be involved in trying this with someone? What is the best outcome that could happen? What is the worst that could happen?

Action Steps to Take

- Get a few 3 × 5 cards and write the following:
  1. "I feel _____
  2. when _____."
- Think through the "I feel" message using the recent situation in which you were mad.

  First: A—Acknowledge you are/were angry.

  Second: B—Backtrack and identify the primary emotion(s).

  "I feel . . ."

  Third: C—Consider the cause.

  "when . . ."
- Identify two relationships that would benefit by your using the "I feel" statements.
- Ask God to help you be a part of the healing process in those relationships.

10

Frustration from
Unmet Expectations

For people who live on expectations, to face up to
their realization is something of an ordeal.

—Elizabeth Bowen

A few days before my (Chip's) scheduled return home
from a rather long missions trip to the Philippines, we
were told that the airport would be closed to international flights
for three months. Apparently there were some government and
military problems going on. I had already been there for several
weeks and was extremely anxious to get home to my wife and
children. I was really missing them.

So, I started praying—hard—that I might be able to get home.
I didn't want to stay three more months. I remember praying
Psalm 145 over and over again with passion: "Oh God, please
show me your mighty works. Open the door, change my heart,

sovereignly move on my behalf that I might return to family and to my calling at the church."

About a day or so later, there was a little calm, and the government allowed a few planes to go. Fortunately, I was able to get on one. Let me tell you, I didn't complain about the food, about the layovers, or about my baggage getting lost. Why? Because my expectations were low, and they were simple. I wanted to get home. I didn't care how; I just wanted to get home. They could have given me a seat hanging on to the wing, and I would have been thankful. The plane was packed with smoking, sweaty people. I didn't get much sleep, and the food was terrible. But I was thankful—filled with gratitude because I was on the plane. And my low expectations were met: I made it home.

In contrast, however, when we lived in Texas, my family and I made a trip to California. We were trying to save money, so we chose a less expensive airline that didn't have direct flights. I asked if food would be served and was told that it was customary to have a light snack served on each flight. The plane stopped in five or six cities—I lost count. The planes were on schedule, weren't packed with sweaty people, and were clean. We went from early morning until what seemed to be very late at night. But the "snack" consisted of peanuts and a drink, then pretzels and a drink, then peanuts and a drink, and then pretzels and a drink. We hadn't eaten anything substantial all day and were traveling with three kids. I thought a "light snack" meant a sandwich or something else. The kids were hungry, our ears were popping, and our bodies were worn out. I was tired and I was ticked. My expectations weren't met, so I was mad.

What's the difference between these two airline experiences? On one I was thrilled with poor conditions. On the other I was ticked with good conditions. The only difference was my expectations.

Expectations Fulfilled

We have expectations. Whether spoken or written, clearly stated or vaguely understood, we all have them—lots of them. Our plans have been thwarted, our hopes dashed, and our schedule halted. We say, "Life isn't supposed to be like this!"

When we expect our marriage to be problem-free and happily-ever-after and it's not, we get frustrated. We also get frustrated when we work hard on a project only to have the teacher or boss ask for it to be redone; when we expect the grocery clerk to be efficient and he isn't; when we expect to find an item at the store and discover they're all out; when we attend a meeting and it starts twenty minutes late; when we plan to finish a project in a certain amount of time and it takes longer. Big or small, significant or insignificant, it doesn't matter, frustration arises when our expectations aren't met.

Feeling frustrated often results in getting angry, regardless of whether the obstacle in our way is real or perceived. It can come from an event, the traffic, a clerk, a long wait in line, the economy, or a person. Whatever the source, if we aren't being treated as expected, if we aren't getting to do what we thought we could do, we get frustrated.

If we expect life to be fair and discover it's not, we can become bitter. If we expect others to treat us with dignity and respect, we become incensed when someone is rude or discourteous. If we expect life to be hassle-free, we become perennial whiners about life's problems. When goals are blocked and life's not going the way we want, we get frustrated.

The problem with having expectations is that

> you assume that people know and accept your rules. When they violate your shoulds [expectations], their behavior seems like a deliberate break with what is correct, intelligent, reasonable, or moral. . . . The problem is that others don't see reality as you do.

Their perception of a situation is colored by their own needs, feelings, and history. . . . So the first problem with shoulds (expectations) is that the people with whom you feel angry rarely agree with you.[1]

We develop bound-to-fail expectations when we make assumptions about others' motives or intentions, when we expect life to be fair and it isn't, when we expect others to read our minds, or when we feel a sense of entitlement to things or behaviors.

A single, thirty-year-old woman came to Becca's office, referred by her pastor. Though she didn't look much older than twenty, she said she had felt depressed for several years. At twenty-five, she met a "wonderful man" and fell in love. They planned to get married the following year, but five months before the wedding, he changed his mind and became more distant. They eventually broke up, and she hadn't seen him for three years. Her depression was fueled by an intense internal anger at herself.

> When our expectations and our life experience don't match up, we become frustrated.

Amid tears, she explained, "I expected him to change his mind again. I expected to be married by thirty. I expected my life to be different." Her inner anger was the result of unfulfilled expectations.

When our expectations and our life experience don't match up, we become frustrated. If life is a little off course, we might tolerate it, but the more our plans miss the mark, the more anger grows. If you think this is something unique to our day, think again. This issue of expectations and anger are as old as human nature itself. This is illustrated powerfully in a classic passage from the Old Testament.

Naaman's Expectations

In 2 Kings 5, there's a story about a man named Naaman. He was commander of the army for the king of Aram and highly regarded in the sight of his master. Whenever he went out to battle, he was victorious. He was a valiant soldier, but he had a problem. He suffered from leprosy.

The king's servant girl told him about a godly prophet in Israel named Elisha. She had heard that Elisha did some amazing things and thought that perhaps he could heal Naaman. This valiant soldier went to the king of Israel and requested that he be healed. Though the king of Israel became concerned—he feared retaliation or war if Naaman wasn't healed—Elisha heard about the situation and sent a message telling the king not to worry. He invited Naaman to come see him.

Naaman, in the meantime, had developed some expectations. He had preconceived ideas of what should happen. He expected this well-known prophet to personally greet him, acknowledge his importance, and have an elaborate ceremony in which to conduct the healing. But that isn't what happened at all.

So Naaman went with his horses and chariots and stopped at the door of Elisha's house. Elisha sent a messenger to say to him, "Go, wash yourself seven times in the Jordan, and your flesh will be restored and you will be cleansed."

But Naaman went away *angry* and said, "*I thought* that he would surely come out to me and stand and call on the name of the LORD his God, wave his hand over the spot and cure me of my leprosy. Are not Abana and Pharpar, the rivers of Damascus, better than any of the waters of Israel? Couldn't I wash in them and be cleansed?" So he turned and went off in a rage.

Naaman's servants went to him and said, "My father, if the prophet had told you to do some great thing, would you not have done it? How much more, then, when he tells you, 'Wash and be cleansed!'"

So he went down and dipped himself in the Jordan seven times, as the man of God had told him, and his flesh was restored and became clean like that of a young boy.

Then Naaman and all his attendants went back to the man of God. He stood before him and said, "Now I know that there is no God in all the world except in Israel." (2 Kings 5:9–15, emphasis added)

As we read, Naaman went to Elisha's house and was given a message. Elisha didn't go to meet him in person. Naaman was told to wash himself and be on his way—nothing elaborate or spectacular. Naaman went away enraged because things didn't go as he expected. Elisha didn't come out to greet him, didn't wave his hand, didn't ceremoniously cry aloud to God. Naaman didn't like the river chosen, the method chosen, nor the means chosen. He says (v. 11), "I thought . . . ," which indicates an expectation. He was mad because he assumed how things would be done, how Elisha and God should work.

Fortunately, Naaman had a bold servant who said something along the lines of, "If the prophet had told you to do something extravagant, you would have done it, right? If he'd asked you to stand on your head in the corner or walk around in circles and whistle, you would have. So why don't you just do what he said? What do you have to lose?" So Naaman went down to the Jordan River, dipped himself seven times, as the man of God had told him, and was miraculously healed of leprosy. This is one of the most graphic examples in Scripture of how our expectations can cause incredible anger. Namaan had predecided what Elisha and God were supposed to do. His anger from unmet expectations almost prevented him from being healed of a disgusting lifelong disease.

What About You?

What are *your* expectations? What do you expect from family members and friends? What assumptions do you have about your job, your marriage, your kids, and your parents? What are your expectations for your life? What have you predetermined about your marriage, your ministry, your money? Are they realistic and God-guided? Or are they too rigid, too lofty, or too difficult? If the latter, you may be setting yourself up for misery, heartache, and anger.

In the life of faith, there's always a tension between being realistic and believing that God will do some amazing things in your life. When you have great faith for the things he has promised, your expectations should be high. But many people have false expectations—high hopes with no realistic basis—and end up disappointed. That's where you'll need to be careful. When your expectations and reality don't mix, you may get angry. That's a signal to you that there's a problem. Remember, the problem is not anger but your hurt and frustration from unmet needs and expectations.

> Letting other people know what you expect of them is a characteristic of the most productive relationships and effective organizations. Letting people know what is expected of them gives them the opportunity to validate whether or not your expectation is realistic—if they feel they can meet it. If they think they can't, they are able to explain their viewpoint, and together you can reach a "realistic expectation." This prevents you from having unrealistically high expectations of others, and saves you from needless and unjust anger.[2]

Make your expectations realistic—as God defines "realistic," not as others do. They should be achievable, attainable, and applicable. If they don't fit, then they should be discarded or placed on another person or situation. I don't expect my youngest child to keep up with her older sister, because that would be unfair. And yet that's what many of us tend to do. We place expectations on people and situations unfairly. Your expectations need to be correctly applied and realistically appropriate.

In addition to expecting a lot from others, many or perhaps most of us also expect too much from ourselves. We assume we should understand, do, or be something we don't understand, can't do, or aren't meant to be. We get down on ourselves for not living up to our own ideals. We conduct inner whipping sessions and are far too hard on ourselves. When this happens, of course, anger is close at hand—inward anger that results in depression or outward anger that results in aggression.

Expectations Become Demands

Expectations easily turn into demands. Instead of "I would *like* such and such to happen," all too often we find ourselves *expecting* it to happen. When it doesn't and our demand is thwarted, we get mad. Assumptions about our relationships, our fulfillment, our job, our marriages, and our spirituality subtly slide into demands and commands.

Watch out when you find yourself using such words as *ought, should, must, always,* and *never.* "You *should* do this or that. You *must* be more sensitive. Our children *ought* to be more responsible. You *never* give me your attention. My job *should* be exciting." These words can be reliable indicators that our expectations may have been transformed into demands. When our desires don't come through, we get disappointed; but when our demands don't come through, we get mad.

> **Watch out when you find yourself using such words as *ought, should, must, always,* and *never.***

The first time a certain fifty-year-old man came to Becca's office for counseling, he made it clear that he wanted results. His words seemed to imply, "I don't want to waste my time or money, so you'd better be good!" He referred to himself as "extremely frustrated" and shied away from using the word "angry." As he shared why he came to counseling, he frequently used the words *expected, should have,* and *their responsibility.* It became clear he had many expectations on the people around him, both at home and at work. He was frustrated because others didn't respond the way he thought they should or do things he considered to be their responsibility. When asked if he had communicated his expectations, he responded, "But they should know. It's obvious." It was clear why he was frustrated.

After hearing an overview of his concerns during that initial session, I directly addressed his expectations of me. "What do you expect me to do for you? I don't know you—how you think, what you want, what you need. So let's talk about your expectations of me." As we talked, I clarified what I could and couldn't do, in which areas I felt I could be of assistance and in which areas I could not. I discussed what he could expect and not expect, encouraging him to openly communicate any frustrations he might have with me and/or what I was doing. In so doing, I provided a model for communicating—clarifying expectations—and, I hope, laid the groundwork for him to have at least one relationship in which expectations were out in the open.

Tool #2: Communicating Frustration

The simple tool for communicating our frustration from unmet expectations is to change our demand statements to desire statements. "*I desire* a fulfilling marriage. *I wish* our children were more responsible. *It would be nice if* the house could be clean more often. *I hope* to get good grades in school. *It would be wonderful* if our families could get together and have a peaceful holiday." Instead of "I expect," "I want," and "I demand," we say "I desire," "I wish," and "I hope."

> The simple tool for communicating our frustration from unmet expectations is to change our demand statements to desire statements.

Anytime we place demands on situations and on others, the whole system is bound to fail, because we can't control situations, God, or those around us. *We need to shift our shoulds, oughts, and musts to hopes, wishes, and desires.*

So far we've learned to stop and ask ourselves what we're feeling and why. We've also learned that we need to communicate our needs to others in ways that are clear and nonthreatening. Now we can build on what we learned in the last chapter about making "I feel" statements by adding "I desire."

Broken down, it has three parts:

1. "I feel _____ (underlying emotion)
2. when _____. (what happened)
3. I wish (hope, desire, would like) _____." (what we wish were different)

> "I wish so-and-so liked me and wanted to be my friend." "I wish I could get ahead financially." "I wish I were a better mom." "I hope our family can get along better." "I would like to get a better job." "It would be nice, Lord, if my body worked better." "I wish you would treat the rest of the family with more kindness."

When we incorporate all of these, we may find ourselves making statements like:

- "I feel taken for granted when you come home late. I wish you would make an effort to be on time."
- "I feel lonely when you're gone on trips. I wish you had a different job."
- "I feel jealous when Bobby gets more of your time than I do. I would like us to spend more time alone together."
- "I feel ashamed when I can't get the house clean enough. I would like to know what you expect."

When we learn to use this simple three-part tool, we communicate in ways that build rather than break relationships.

The Bottom Line

When what we expect and what we experience are too dissimilar, we get mad. For our expectations to be realistic, they must be attainable, applicable, and achievable. When we find ourselves using such words as *ought, should, must, always,* and *never,* watch out. They are good indicators that our expectations may have been transformed into demands.

Questions to Consider

1. What are some of your unspoken expectations for those around you—friends, spouse, children, boss, employees, pastor, leaders, etc.?
2. Do you think some of your expectations might be unrealistic? Which ones? With whom?
3. Do you have some unrealistic expectations on yourself—to be perfect, to never make a mistake, to fulfill everyone's needs, to have regular devotions early in the morning with two small children, etc.?

Action Steps to Take

- Get a few 3 × 5 cards and write the following:
  1. "I feel _____
  2. when _____.
  3. I wish (desire, hope, would like) _____."
- Think through a situation in which you got mad in terms of this three-part message. Identify how your expectations

(for yourself or others) might become more attainable, applicable, and achievable by approaching conflict this way.

- Ask yourself, "Who or what really frustrates me and why?" The distance between your expectations and your experience is frustration. Write in a journal or notebook what this question has helped you discover about your unspoken and/or unconscious expectations.

11

Insecurity from Threatened Esteem

> Security is not the absence of danger, but the
> presence of God no matter the danger.

I (Becca) was counseling a woman who had two young children. She wanted help with low self-esteem, and one week she seemed especially irritated. A neighbor had "insinuated that I'm a bad mom!" The neighbor had asked her to tell her children not to throw things over the fence into her yard. "She's saying I can't control my kids, that I'm not supervising them very well. She thinks I'm irresponsible." Fortunately, she was soon able to acknowledge that her anger was really fueled by her own insecurities. She admitted that her neighbor had not implied anything about her parenting skills and had, in fact, asked her in a congenial, polite way. She eventually acknowledged that her anger reaction was triggered by feelings of insecurity.

When our safety, abilities, role, or personality is threatened or questioned, we often respond in anger. The root emotion, however, is insecurity. Unfortunately, it's a part of each of us.

Our feelings of insecurity may arise from an unappreciative boss or spouse, derogatory comments about our abilities, or the endangerment of our family. It happens when our job is at stake, our children are physically harmed, our character is slandered, our home is foreclosed, our business goes bankrupt, our secrets are made public, our intelligence is minimized, or our looks go unnoticed. When these kinds of things happen, we feel threatened and insecure, which then leads to anger. Though anger shows on the surface, insecurity lies beneath it.

What do we mean by "threatened self or situation"? This occurs when our self-worth is attacked, our character is questioned, or our abilities are undervalued. It happens when we don't feel esteemed, respected, or appreciated. The result is that we feel insecure. Insecurity also occurs when we and/or people we love are in some sort of danger, whether emotionally or physically. A "threatened situation," then, is whenever people or things we value are under attack or in danger.

Some of the threats that cause insecurity come *physically*. When another driver dangerously cuts us off, when we read of kidnappings, when we hear of molestation, rape, and assault, we feel insecure living in this uncontrollable, scary world. Our inner feelings generally come to the surface as protective, fear-driven anger.

Most threats to our self-worth or well-being come *verbally*. Proverbs 15:1 reminds us, "A gentle answer turns away wrath, but a harsh word stirs up anger." Wise old Solomon knew that unkind words stir up the anger stew. Have you ever heard someone say things like, "Is that the best you can do?" "Is that what you're going to wear?" "Aren't you going to do anything about the situation?" "Can't you figure it out?" "What's wrong with you?" "I thought you were smarter than that." Or what about when those you love are devalued or demeaned? "That was *your* kid who did such and such?" "Maybe your child should be on another team." "I can't believe what your spouse did—now *that* was stupid." "Maybe your child should be held back a year." "He did *that* to you?" Name-calling, criticism, impatience, intolerance, put-downs, and petty talk all produce anger because they threaten who we are, what we do, and what we value. They attack our character, our commitments, and those we cherish.

> Name-calling, criticism, impatience, intolerance, put-downs, and petty talk all produce anger because they threaten who we are, what we do, and what we value.

Those harsh words stir up anger because anytime we feel like someone or something is threatening who we are, what we do, or what we have, anger jumps in to protect and preserve. The saying "Sticks and stones may break my bones but words will never hurt me" is untrue. Words hurt deeply. The wounds and scars often remain for life.

When your little ones come home from school and tell you that someone called them a name—a nerd, a wimp, a scaredy-cat, a sissy, or stupid—it stings. It's an attack on their personal worth. That's why kids get into fights on playgrounds. That's why we get into fights as grown-ups.

Harsh words cut us deeply, leaving permanent scars. They make us angry because they make us insecure. Unfortunately, when we feel threatened or under attack, we either retreat and withdraw from people or gear up for battle and fight back.

But Proverbs warns us: "An offended brother is more unyielding than a fortified city" (Prov. 18:19). We are urged not to become unyielding, unforgiving people. We are also urged not to offend others. Unforgiveness easily turns us into grudge holders. We hang on to our anger as a means of payback: "Since you hurt me, I'll hurt you." Instead of seeking reconciliation, we've decided to stay mad. We fortify and alienate ourselves from others. When we fight back and attack a person's worth, we may offend them so deeply they become unable to yield or forgive. We set a vicious cycle in motion in which two people begin fortifying their walls until they can no longer communicate with each other.

Tool #3: Ask Yourself, "Why Am I Feeling Threatened?"

Those familiar with military operations may recall the course of action when danger threatens. They called it a "Red Alert." It signals everyone to be on their toes, to be alert and ready for action. It is the time to get the adrenaline juices flowing, to be attentive and cautious.

When we feel threatened, we tend to call a Red Alert. Unfortunately, we usually do it automatically, without properly assessing the risk. We do it over small, insignificant things as well as big, overwhelming issues. Whether the impending intruder is a mouse or a monster, we gear up for action with almost the same intensity. We get fuming mad when a stranger flips us off on the highway and when our spouse has been unfaithful, when the store clerk makes a rude comment and when the boss takes credit for all the work we did, when there's a long line at the bank and when we discover our teenager stole some money. We need to stop and assess the situation before we blast in with heavy artillery.

Before we move ahead with some practical ways to address these feelings of insecurity, I (Chip) think it's critical to go on record and say that we're all desperately insecure. Ever since sin entered the world, we have followed the pattern of being afraid that others will see our "nakedness" (the exposed aspects of our lives—emotional, psychological, or physical—that don't measure up). So we hide from one another out of fear and shame.

117

It's critical to go on record and say that we're all desperately insecure.

One of the most liberating experiences of my life was reading a book by Swiss psychologist Paul Tournier called *The Strong and the Weak*. In it he makes the case that we are all desperately insecure and reveal it by either *strong* reactions—powering up, bragging, exploding, name-dropping, seeking to impress—or by *weak* reactions—withdrawing, being excessively shy, having a victim mentality, putting ourselves down, having low self-esteem, refusing to try because we know we'll fail. In both cases, the goal is to keep others at a distance and protect ourselves from being exposed, assuming we won't measure up and will be rejected.

To openly and honestly admit my insecurity has helped me to be far less threatened and really use the following tools outlined in this chapter.

How can you assess volatile situations in your life? First, try to identify the primary emotions beneath your anger. "What am I really feeling?" If you discover that you feel insecure and threatened, ask yourself the following questions:

1. What is being threatened? Why do I feel insecure? (What is under attack?)

What is under attack? Is it my character, my pride, my family, my values, my job, my possessions, the safety of myself or a loved one, my self-worth, my intelligence, my looks? Am I being overly defensive about a personal weakness, or am I feeling unjustly accused or unfairly treated? Am I being personally threatened, or am I being adversely affected by someone else's bad mood or by their indiscriminate negative words or deeds? Is there an area in my life that needs some work? Am I feeling insecure about one of my weaknesses? If so, I need to improve so my insecurities don't lead me to make an angry fool of myself.

2. Who is involved? (Who is attacking me?)

When we realize that the root reason is insecurity, we need to stop and ask ourselves, "Who is attacking me? Who's involved?" Is it the ill-mannered stranger on the highway, or is it a loving friend? Is this a vengeful coworker or an objective outsider? Is it a crude clerk or a caring counselor?

Every day, a man bought a newspaper from the same grouchy salesman. One day the man was accompanied by a colleague while buying a paper. The colleague asked, "How do you put up with such rude behavior day after day? Doesn't it make you mad?" The man replied, "I decided long ago that I'm not going to let anyone else determine how my day will be." He wasn't about to let the grump behind the counter decide how he would feel.

3. Is the threat significant or insignificant? (Is the attack menial or meaningful?)

Is this really worth fighting for? Is this a mountain or a molehill? Is this an actual or perceived threat? Am I blowing it out of proportion? Should I ignore it and let it go? Do I need to gain perspective? If we discover the threat to be unimportant and the person peripheral, we should abandon our anger.

4. Whose approval am I seeking? From where does my security come? (Why do I feel attacked?)

Do others' words and actions easily make me feel insecure? Do I worry too much about what other people say or think? Am I secure in Christ, or am I seeking approval from others? Am I assured of his sovereignty, goodness, and love? As we answer penetrating questions like these, our anger often fades away. We begin to realize the significance we foolishly placed on something insignificant. Priorities come into focus, and we consciously decide not to let others ruin our day or our lives. Doing so is an act of our will. We choose to let go of the anger and let God show us where better to place our emotional energies.

Finding Our Security

What can you do to get out of this maze? You can affirm your security in Christ. He knows each one of us individually and personally.

> We choose to let go of the anger and let God show us where better to place our emotional energies.

He knows your faults, weaknesses, and insecurities yet loves you continually, completely, and unconditionally. You can find unfailing love, grace, and mercy in him. Though people may speak ill of you, and though life's woes encompass you, you can find rest in him. He knows that we are human, prone to insecurity, pride, and problems. Still, he loves us.

When you find your security in Christ, you're less burdened by your own failings and less bothered by what others say or do. You'll be less likely to stoop to retaliation. You'll sleep better and keep your mind filled with goodness. As we're commanded, "Whatever is true, whatever is noble, whatever is right, whatever is pure, whatever is lovely, whatever is admirable—if anything is excellent or praiseworthy—think about such things. . . . And the God of peace will be with you" (Phil. 4:8–9).

It's important to be able to say to yourself, "I'm secure in Christ. What that person thinks about me is irrelevant. I'm not going to stoop to behaving like that. If I hear someone talking about me at work—or worse, at church—I won't seek revenge. If they gossip about me and say things that aren't true, I won't get out my anger weapons. I will seek to have God's loving, forgiving heart."

We can guarantee that people will attack you or let you down sometimes. We all get hurt, and we all get frustrated. Your needs and expectations will not always be met. At times you will be threatened and feel insecure. These things are a given in life.

There's only one person in the entire universe who knows how to meet our needs and heal our hurts. Only one person always fulfills the expectations he has for us. And when we're feeling insecure and afraid, only one person sees all our inadequacies and imperfections and loves us still—just the

> Our inner feelings of insecurity generally come to the surface as protective, fear-driven anger.

way we are. That's the glory of the cross. That's the message of New Testament Christianity.

The Bottom Line

Our inner feelings of insecurity generally come to the surface as protective, fear-driven anger. In these last three chapters, we've learned that we need to look below the surface of our anger and ask ourselves, "What is the root cause?"

What's Underneath My Anger?

1. Am I hurt from unmet needs?
   Has someone rejected me? Do I feel guilty? Abandoned? Lonely? Rejected? Betrayed?
2. Am I feeling frustrated from unmet expectations?
   Do I feel let down? Did I fail? Did something fall through? Were my expectations realistic?
3. Am I feeling insecure from being threatened?
   Was my self-worth attacked? My character questioned? My abilities undervalued? Did I feel disrespected or unappreciated? Why do I feel insecure? What's being threatened? Who's involved? Is the threat significant or insignificant? Whose approval am I seeking? From where does my security come?

Questions to Consider

1. When was the last time you got angry when your skills or self-esteem felt threatened?

2. Who in your life especially triggers your feelings of inadequacy? What principles shared in this chapter can most help you minimize the impact of their behavior and words on your self-worth?
3. Which of your attitudes and behaviors do you think would change most if you felt fully secure in Christ?

Action Steps to Take

- Think of a recent time when your anger was fueled by your insecurities. Ask yourself:

    1. What is being threatened? Why do I feel insecure? (What is under attack?)
    2. Who is involved? (Who is attacking me?)
    3. Is the threat significant or insignificant? (Is the attack menial or meaningful?)
    4. Whose approval am I seeking? (From where does my security come?)

    What new things did you learn about yourself? Do you tend to go to "Red Alert" too quickly and with the same intensity, regardless of whether the threat is small or substantial? Are you secure in Christ?

- Choose a safe friend or colleague and share with that person a skill or responsibility about which you have been insecure. Notice afterward whether your honesty feels stressful or liberating.
- Practice a new mind-set this week. Remind yourself periodically that each person you speak with is basically insecure. At the end of the week, share with a trusted friend how that knowledge changed the tone of your conversations.

PART 4

TURNING ANGER FROM A FOE TO A FRIEND

12

The Anger ABCDs

Your temper is one of your most valuable possessions. Don't lose it.

In chapter 7, I (Chip) shared the story of an angry outburst at my wife and children after some unmet needs that occurred the night before. I had been teaching this material on anger at the time, and something amazing happened. After my outbursts I sat in the driveway with the car running. I knew I was angry. I also knew that the root of my anger at my wife was my feeling of loneliness. "What's going on here?" I asked myself, and then, a little later, "What am I going to do about it now?" In the span of those minutes in the car, I went from fuming mad to figuring out the *what* and *why* of my anger. Once I did that, I could try to determine the best way to deal with the mess I'd gotten myself into. This is an example of the Anger ABCDs.

As we've seen, the Anger ABCDs guide us in dealing with anger in a simple and easy-to-remember way. They encourage us to examine our anger, to identify what lies below, to consider the contributing factors, and then to determine how best to deal with it. We have found, both personally and professionally, that using the Anger ABCDs can help! They've been used successfully by many fellow anger strugglers.

The Anger ABCDs

When anger arises we need to:

    A Acknowledge (admit and accept) the anger.
    B Backtrack to the root reasons of the anger.
    C Consider the cause (contributing factors) of the anger.
    D Determine how best to deal with the anger.

Let's go through each step, focusing primarily on the last step.

A—Acknowledge

We begin by acknowledging, accepting, and admitting that we feel angry. We don't stuff it or pretend it's not there. We don't deny its existence but come to grips with the fact that we are ticked off. This will be a hard task for those who grew up in homes where anger was viewed as a terrible monster or a sin, or for those in environments that frown upon any expression of displeasure. "If your parents didn't allow you to see their expressions of anger, your ideas about this emotion are probably confused. . . . You grew up with no model for understanding your own anger. You had no label for it. You had no way of knowing how to express it or respond to it."[1] Before we can begin to deal effectively with our anger, we must admit it's there and look it right in the eyes. We have to stop running from it.

B—Backtrack to the Primary Emotion

We've already identified the common emotions underlying anger. When we backtrack, we seek to find out what emotion preceded our anger. We get our fingers dirty and dig underneath the anger in order to discover the root. We ask ourselves, "Why am I angry? What am I *really* feeling? What is the root reason for my anger? Am I feeling jealousy, fear, shame, grief, hopelessness, rejection, loneliness, anxiety, worthlessness, pride, envy, or a sense of being trapped?" We become self-investigators in order to uncover the root emotion.

C—Consider the Cause

When we consider the cause, we take a look at whatever factors contributed to why we feel the way we do. There are two ways to consider the cause—one is linked to the present, the other to the past. In the present, we identify what happened. Did someone insult us, forget something important to us, arrive late, not include us, endanger us? Those who don't mind introspection can also consider what factors in our past contributed to our current feelings of anger. In an earlier chapter, we read about the various factors that affect our responses. We learned that our anger is affected by our personalities, past, culture, current situation, age, and gender. It can be helpful to return to these areas to see if they are contributing to our feelings. Did something or someone in my past trigger the anger? Am I carrying over remnants from ages past? Am I angry at a cultural expectation, a gender-role stereotype, a physical limitation, a financial restriction, or an ethnic bias?

Though it is good to consider the causes, we want to be careful not to get bogged down in introspection. We need to spend most of our time on the D of the Anger ABCDs.

D—Determine How Best to Deal with It

When angry, we need to determine how best to deal with the situation. Our goal is best summarized in Ephesians 4:26: "In your anger do not sin." We need to know how to be angry appropriately, without sinning. (For some, after an angry outburst, D may symbolize the need to determine how to deal with the damage done.) In order to make a good decision, we need to have the right reason and the right response. This process requires both discernment and wisdom.

The right reason forces us to examine our motives. Are we angry for righteous or self-righteous reasons, for good or bad reasons? The primary way to determine this is through honest conversations with God and some honest personal inventory.

Having the right response requires that we determine whether or not to confront, when to confront, and how to confront. We need to decide what we are going to do about our feelings and/or the situation and then decide on the best course of action (or inaction).

In order to help you sort through this sometimes complex set of feelings, we need to consider the who, what, how, and when of the situation. First, here's a quick overview:

The Who, What, How, and When of Determining How to Deal with Anger

Who? *At whom* am I really angry? Myself? Someone else? The situation? God?

What? *What* should I do? Express directly or release indirectly? (Confront or conceal?) Will my plans make matters worse or make them better?

How? *How* do I deal with the situation? In person? On the phone? Through a letter? And/or engage in anger discharge activities?

When? *When* should I deal with the situation? Now, later, or never?

Who?

At whom am I really angry? Myself? Someone else? The situation? God?

128

At whom is the anger really directed? Is it directed at a particular person, or is that person just a scapegoat or an easy target? Is our anger actually directed at God? At ourselves? Several years ago in counseling, a young woman was dealing with intense anger. Against her protests, she had been date-raped. When we considered the true focus of her anger, she realized for the first time that she felt more anger at herself than at the rapist. That isn't uncommon. Others acknowledge deep anger at God for their situation. It may sound simple, but only when you honestly come to grips with the one you're really angry at can genuine healing occur.

Next, determine who is involved. Is the person significant in my life? Do their opinions matter to me? Am I overly dependent on what they think of me or of their opinion? Is this the first or the hundredth time this person has done something that bothers me? Do they remind me of someone in my past toward whom I still harbor anger? (We often get angry at people because they remind us of someone else.) Am I extra mad because of a previous offense that hasn't been resolved? Am I really mad at myself? Have I unfairly directed my anger at someone? Slowly read these questions again, but this time read them as they relate to a recent relational conflict. As you ask yourself these penetrating questions, listen quietly to what begins to surface in your heart.

> **Only when you honestly come to grips with the one you're really angry at can genuine healing occur.**

What?

What should I do? *What* are my options?

What should we do about the situation? What should we do about our feelings? Should I express my concerns directly to the person(s) involved (confront)? Should I redirect and release my anger (conform and conceal or quit)? Will my plans escalate and perpetuate the situation, or will they dissipate it? (Will it make matters worse or make it better?)

When we find ourselves in an unwanted situation with angry feelings, we basically have two choices: Do I *express my feelings directly* to the person, or do I *release them indirectly* through various activities? Does the situation require concerns to be communicated directly to the person(s) involved? Or is it better to redirect anger elsewhere, finding alternative, healthy, non-destructive, nonconfrontational ways to express it?

Dealing with it directly means choosing to confront the situation. We try and change it. We act rather than acquiesce. We take action and appropriately let the persons involved know about our anger and its root emotions, what contributed to their existence, and what we would like to be different. It's best to express ourselves clearly without blaming or attacking. We let our anger be known, but in ways we previously discussed. "I feel _____ when _____. I wish _____." We get it out wisely and carefully, never impulsively or without considering the consequences and casualties.

Dealing with our anger indirectly gives us a few more choices. Sometimes it's best to accept things the way they are (conform) and not to share our anger with those involved (conceal). But it's important to make sure our motivation isn't from an uncomfortable situation. We choose this option not by default or out of hopelessness, but out of a calculated conclusion that it would be best not to stir the waters or rock the boat at this particular time in this specific situation. Wisdom sometimes demands that we choose not to reprove someone when past history or other circumstances dictate it to be an exercise in futility (Prov. 9:8–9). Sometimes it's best to walk away.

We may have to find a new job, do business with a different company, or discontinue an unhealthy friendship. We choose not to confront but to quit. We should consider this only after we have weighed all other options carefully and determined that letting go is the best course of action.

To *redirect and release* our anger means keeping it to ourselves. We've examined our motives, thought through the situation, and decided it would be best not to communicate our feelings to those involved. So how is this different from bottling up or stuffing anger—suppressing and repressing and pretending it doesn't exist? When redirecting our anger, we acknowledge it and look for healthy, nondestructive ways to get it out. We transfer the anger into some kind of action or activity.

When deciding whether to deal with the concern directly or indirectly, we must then consider whether our way of dealing with the problem is going to *escalate and perpetuate* our anger or help *dissipate* or dissolve it away. Not long ago I (Becca) was feeling intense anger at a community leader. At first I kept my frustrations to myself. Slowly, however, the anger oozed out until I finally began openly expressing my disapproval. Each time I expressed my frustration I noticed that I felt worse, not better. Communicating my anger hadn't been cathartic and helpful, it had been detrimental and destructive—mainly for myself. Expressing myself actually fed my anger, causing it to escalate and perpetuate.

> When redirecting our anger, we acknowledge it and look for healthy, nondestructive ways to get it out.

Research indicates that expressing anger often makes it worse. The more anger we communicate, the angrier we feel. For some, expressing it can help get it off their chest and lessen the load, but for most of us, it stirs us up rather than calming us down. This is very important to consider when we're deciding what to do.

How?

> *How* do I deal with the situation? In person?
> On the phone? Through a letter? Engage in
> anger discharge activities?

If we decide to deal directly with those involved, we must determine how best to do it. So often we come to the right conclusion about *what* to do in a situation but then fail to know *how* to do it. Let me (Becca) share a few ways I've helped my clients over the years when they ask, "How do I best confront this person with whom I have unresolved anger?"

Expressing Directly

In person. Most of the time it's best to go directly to the person involved. If he or she is nearby and available, it's generally better to do it face-to-face. Though this may be uncomfortable, it allows full communication through body language and gestures. Both parties can respond back and forth, explain misunderstandings, and reply. It invites open dialogue rather than a one-sided communication of concerns.

In counseling, I have found it very helpful to have people role-play the interaction before they carry it out. Sometimes I ask them to communicate their concerns to an empty chair. Other times I ask them to switch seats and respond as if they are the other person. Occasionally I will play one of the people—either the one who feels offended or the person the client is mad at—and the client plays the other part. Role-playing helps prepare us for the confrontation, anticipate possible responses, and develop empathy as to why the other person did or said what they did.

Before any type of direct expression of anger, it's wise to try to put ourselves in the other person's place. We usually gain a greater understanding and sometimes greater compassion. It's also wise to write out and clarify our concerns ahead of time. Before putting our foot in our mouth, we need to go through the Anger ABCDs to determine what's really behind the anger, why it's there, and what we wish were different.

It is also important to remember to use a calm voice, to avoid emotionally laden words (such as cussing, blaming, limiting, or sarcasm), and to remain rational. We must state our concerns clearly, keeping to the facts. We identify our root emotion and what happened without letting anger take over the interaction.

Sometimes it's best to let the person know we want to talk with them. If appropriate, we could even inform them of the area of concern. This allows the person time to think through the situation and, hopefully, to let down defenses. When we confront someone without warning, they are often caught off guard, aren't able to think things through, and make hurtful, defensive statements. But with some, the warning only gives them time to gather ammunition. We need to pray, asking for discernment as to whether to give advanced warning.

By phone. When communicating concerns in person isn't possible, or when it's simply unwise or even dangerous, talking on the phone may be the best method. As with face-to-face conversation, it allows an ongoing give and take. It gives the person the opportunity to respond to our concerns (or accusations). It may be more comfortable or more convenient.

In a letter. When it's unsafe, inadvisable, or impossible to deal with the problem in person, then we may choose to communicate our concerns in written form. Putting our concerns down in writing forces us to clarify them, keeps us from rambling, prevents the other person from hijacking or side-tracking the conversation, and helps us avoid expressing our anger in destructive ways. We may go through several drafts before reaching the final letter, but ideally, by then, we've cooled down, realized our part in the problem, and sifted out our accusatory, negative counterattacks.

When writing a letter, it's extremely wise to ask an objective outsider to read it before sending it. Ask the person to be brutally honest in their appraisal of the situation and the letter. Graciously accept their recommendations. Ask them how the letter might be misinterpreted or misunderstood, where it might be off base or pity driven, and where it might be too forceful or demanding.

When Abraham Lincoln was president, Secretary Stanton was furious because an officer had disobeyed or failed to comprehend an order. Lincoln advised him, "Write him now while you have it on your mind. Make it sharp. Cut him all up."

Stanton didn't need much prodding. He wrote a powerfully demeaning letter. When he read it to the president, Lincoln responded, "That's a good one."

Stanton then asked, "By whom can I send the letter?"

"Send it?" replied Lincoln. "Why, don't send it at all. Tear it up. You have freed your mind on the subject, and that is all that is necessary. Tear it up. You never want to send such letters; I never do."

Yes, there are times when it is best to throw the letter away after it has been written. It is always advisable to wait several days before sending an anger-driven letter. By then, we may come to our senses and decide not to send it at all, or we may want to rewrite it in less critical terms.

Expressing Indirectly

If we decide that it's best not to communicate our concerns directly to the person, we may need to identify ways to redirect or release the anger. There are many, many things we can do to vent our pent-up emotions. Here's a list of some of the physically active and emotionally calming activities we can do to get the anger out. We call them Anger Discharge Activities.

Anger Discharge Activities: Physically Active Options

When I (Becca) was young, I saved some money and, with my parents' help, bought my own drum set. (I was a fan of Karen Carpenter, who, you may recall, began as a drummer.) I was the drummer for the high school jazz band as well as for a local rock band. Whenever I was mad about something, I would go and beat those drums over and over again, getting out my negativity. It worked. I usually felt better afterward, not as uptight. In college, when I didn't have drums around, I found that going down to the racquetball court and hitting the ball as hard as I could achieved the same release (and I didn't have to chase the balls very far in the enclosed court). At that time, I needed to do something more physically active to get my pent-up emotions out.

Some people beat their small house rugs, accomplishing two tasks at once—getting out the anger and getting out the dirt (dirty anger?). Pulling weeds, mopping floors, chopping wood, crushing soda cans, and kneading bread are other dual-purpose tasks.

Many find running to be a wonderful option. It's quick and easy, and requires little equipment. But almost any sport can do. How about swimming? In graduate school, I did an extensive paper on stress management. One of the things I remember most was an article about the amazing power of immersion. The author said that when you're stressed, overwhelmed, or frustrated, it helps to go jump in a lake. Whether just jumping in or doing laps, swimming can be incredibly helpful. It's refreshing and invigorating—certainly physically, but perhaps also because it's somewhat like baptism and symbolizes rebirth. Others view it as a cleansing that washes the anger away.

When choosing to release your anger in physically active ways, be careful not to overdo it or to do anything that could be potentially damaging or harmful. Going one hundred miles per hour down the road may make some less angry, but it could also have deadly results. Those prone to violence should use alternative techniques, as physical activities can cause anger to escalate rather than dissipate.

Anger Discharge Activities: Emotionally Calming Options

Thomas Jefferson suggested counting to ten when you're angry. Often enough, that helps. If you get to ten and you're still fuming, count to one hundred. It's also helpful to take a walk, especially in an open space like a park, along the beach, or near a vista point. Seeing a great expanse often helps us get our anger into perspective. Grandeur or vast openness often helps our problems seem smaller.

Writing in a journal provides the opportunity to "get it out" in a healthy way. Some of us have personalities with a greater need to express what we're feeling and thinking. Unfortunately, many think that "getting it off your chest" can only be accomplished when directing at the person you're mad at. But as with a letter you never send, writing out your frustrations in a journal can also achieve this. You also may want to get a tape recorder, go to a mirror, or get a large stuffed animal in order to "tell the person off" and communicate your concerns.

Some of us find it helpful to go for a drive or take a walk. Getting farther away than the next room is sometimes necessary to get a new perspective. Many take a bath to soothe their nerves, calm their emotions, or wash away their negative feelings. A hot bath works for some, while others may need to take a cold shower. For yet others, sitting down with a cup of coffee or tea helps to calm the heart and rest the soul.

Relaxation and breathing techniques can also have a calming effect. So can soothing music. When I feel overwhelmed and easily agitated by the children, I fix a cup of my favorite tea and listen to Gregorian chants. It can work wonders, even in only five minutes.

Before all of this, of course, comes prayer. You might pray something like, "God, I know it's easy for me to make a real fool of myself and do something dumb. I need your perspective and your help."

What do you do to help anger get out constructively rather than destructively? Can you identify those things that help you release it? In counseling, I recommend making a list of possible things to do when you need to vent. Taking a bath or writing in a journal just doesn't do it for some people; they need physical activity. Some people need action, some need reflection. What do *you* need?

The Anger Expression Continuum—"In Your Anger Do Not Sin"

The following continuum depicts the extremes in expressing anger along with a summary of the preferred middle ground.

Continuum of Ways to Express Anger

Unhealthy	Healthy	Healthy	Unhealthy
Get it all out	Express	Redirect and Release	Grin and bear it
Explode	Communicate directly	Discharge indirectly	Implode
Yell, scream, belittle	In person, phone, letter	Physically active or emotionally calming activities	Withdraw, silent treatment

A Word of Warning

While expressing and releasing anger are preferred to imploding and exploding (stuffing or spewing), we must be careful and prayerful to determine which type of expression to use. If God calls us to speak out regarding an injustice, then it would be wrong to get our anger out by going for a jog. Conversely, if we feel we should keep silent and allow the anger an alternative outlet, we should spend time identifying ways to vent it rather than seek opportunities to confront the person.

It's also important to remember that communicating anger directly with someone doesn't always make it go away! *Even when we've gotten it off our chest, it can remain in our heart.* We may also need to engage in activities that help us release the leftover angry energy.

Those are some of the techniques for dealing with our anger, but certainly not all of them. Even so, knowing how to address it is only part of the process. We also need to have a good sense of timing.

When?

> *When* should I deal with the situation? Now, later, or never?

Have you ever watched a surfer? When they choose a wave, their timing must be perfect. Their approach must be precise. If they begin too soon, the wave overthrows them. If they begin too late, the wave passes them by. Timing is everything. Surfers must know when to act if they want their efforts and patience to be rewarded.

But it's not just knowing *when* to catch the particular wave, it's also knowing *whether* to catch the wave. You see, there are waves and then there are *waves*. Surfers must learn to discern which ones to attempt and which to let go by. If they are impatient, they find themselves on a short-lived wave that offers little opportunity to feel the wind and sea dance around them. Sometimes they must wait a long time before the right one comes along.

Timing is likewise crucial when dealing with anger. We need to know when to speak, when to listen, when to confront, when to be silent, when to move forward, and when to retreat. Timing can make or break a relationship. Like the surfer, we need to learn when to proceed and, better yet, whether or not to proceed.

We can deal with our concerns at three possible times: now, later, or never. We need to deal with them now if waiting would likely make matters worse. When emotions are running high, it may be best to let the dust settle and wait until later. In some cases, it may be best never to address the issue, letting time heal the wounds. Most hurt feelings, however, are like open wounds that become infected if left unattended, so this tactic should be used sparingly. Each situation requires much discernment.

> **We can deal with our concerns at three possible times: now, later, or never.**

Ecclesiastes reminds us, "There is a time for everything, and a season for every activity under heaven" (Eccles. 3:1). Our job is to determine when (and whether) to deal with our concerns.

When I (Becca) find myself feeling upset with someone, I try to evaluate whether it is a "time worsens" or a "time heals" situation. If it's a "time worsens" situation, I know that if I don't speak up, the negative feelings inside of me may grow until they erupt disproportionately to the original offense. In this case, I resolve to deal with the problem however unpleasant it might be. If I don't address it, the conflict becomes a major catastrophe.

If it's a "time heals" situation, I tell myself, "I'll wait until some time has gone by before dealing with this one. It's too emotionally charged right now." I realize that it's better to leave it alone for a while; then I'll either get over it or be better able to deal with it once my emotions subside. To confront the person now would only escalate the problem and make matters worse, not better. Sometimes we will need to consider not only the best timing for us but also the best timing for the other person. We may be ready to deal with the situation, but the other person may need more time to cool down or sort things out.

One couple I counseled shared their frustration. "We can't even communicate when we argue." After several questions, we discovered that he was more readily able to sort out and verbalize what was bothering him. The wife, on the other hand, generally needed more time to sift through her thoughts and emotions in order to determine what was at the core of her negative feelings. When they got in a fight, the husband continually pushed for immediate resolution while the wife repeatedly requested "time to sort it out and think it through." His insistence on immediate resolution angered her, and her need to wait and deal with the problem later frustrated him.

Although Becca didn't know it, the last paragraph perfectly describes one of the biggest conflicts Theresa and I had in our marriage. I always wanted to solve it "now," and she always "needed time" to process. We loved each other deeply, but our timing was off. After much discussion, we devised a workable plan that respected both of our needs. Don't underestimate doing things in the right time.

A friend mysteriously stopped speaking to me (Becca) some time ago. Every attempt I made at communicating was met with a cold shoulder, and I didn't know why. I played back our last visits and phone calls in my mind, trying to uncover any insensitivity on my part, but I struck out. A year later, I got a letter explaining how my friend had been upset about something I'd neglected to do. I had no idea of the offense (nor of my friend's expectations) and wasn't even given the opportunity to apologize or explain—until a year later. Now that's bad timing!

When conflicts arise, we tend to gravitate toward extremes. Either we blow up and attack our adversary on the spot, or we retreat in fear of confrontation. Many of us make that decision based on what is most comfortable, not on what is best. An impulsive person may continually choose to deal with their anger immediately because they don't like the ongoing tension and feelings inside. Others choose to avoid any type of confrontation, not because it's the best timing but because it feels safe. They think that ignoring the problem will make it go away. Unfortunately, automatic responses like this generally backfire on you and damage yourself and your relationships even more because you took the comfortable rather than the right road.

If you decide that you aren't running from the situation but do feel that you should wait until a later time to deal with the conflict, you'll probably need to identify ways to vent your negative feelings in healthy, nondestructive ways. You may need to engage in some of those physically active or emotionally calming activities.

> **When conflicts arise, we tend to gravitate toward extremes.**

Like the surfer who must decide if and when to catch a wave, deciding if and when to confront others with our anger and its submerged root emotions takes wisdom and discernment.

Questions to Consider

1. Do you tend to gravitate towards confronting or not confronting when angry? Do you tend to run from confrontation when you shouldn't? Do you tend to confront when you shouldn't?
2. Have you ever written an anger letter? Did you send it? Why/why not? Are you glad you did/didn't?
3. Answer the following questions about the "when" of dealing with your anger:

Do I tend to run from conflict?	Yes	No	Sometimes
Do I tend to immediately attack others during disagreements?	Yes	No	Sometimes
Do I take the time to determine if and when I should deal with a difficulty?	Yes	No	Sometimes
Do I force others into confrontation before they are ready?	Yes	No	Sometimes

Are there any current conflicts I need to face but am avoiding?	Yes	No	Sometimes
Which timing do I favor—*now, later,* or *never?* Why?			

Action Steps to Take

- Make a list of those physically active and emotionally calming activities that you might do when needing to vent your anger elsewhere.
- Think of someone with whom you feel extremely angry. Write a letter to the person. Rewrite it. Keep it in a private place until you feel you should send or destroy it.
- Tell someone about a past confrontation you regret, and describe how you would deal with it differently now.

13

Anger Is a Choice

Two people ought not to get angry at the same time.

Picture this: You're in the middle of a heated, knock-down, drag-out argument with someone—spouse, teenager, friend, roommate, or coworker. On a scale of one to ten, ten being a volcanic eruption, this is about an eight. You blurt out stinging assaults on their competence and take some jabs at their character. You're accusing and attacking. "No, no, no, no!" "What?" "Huh-uh!" "No way!" It's full-blown. You're both going at it full force. The blood is flowing, voices are raised, cutting words are unleashed. Most of us have been there.

Then the phone rings, and you answer it with a cool, calm, collected voice. "Hello, Mom. Oh, I'm fine. How about you?"

Or how about those screaming-turned-serenity moments when you're yelling at the kids and the doorbell rings, or you're arguing at the store and somebody walks by? We go from angry tyrants to lovingly corrective parents. If we can turn off our anger when the phone rings or we're in a public place, then we can turn it off anytime. Anger is a choice.

How we express our anger is a choice. We can choose to let it out in aggressive or assertive ways, in lashing or loving ways. The choice is ours. To say we can't help it isn't true. We have to commit ourselves to well-chosen, premeditated words and take time to ponder, meditate, and contemplate. We need to realize that we have a choice whether to condemn or to consider.

"When frustrated, [many people] assume that anger is the only response possible. This myth leads to the belief that you have no choice. . . . In truth, anger is only one response to frustration. [There is] a whole range of choices and ways to cope when your needs are blocked."[1]

> Nobody *makes* us angry; we choose to feel that way.

Research on anger in other cultures confirms this fact. People from different cultures respond to frustration with submission, contrition, sorrow, withdrawal, or determination. Even within a culture there is a variety of responses available.

The first step in realizing that anger is a choice—*our* choice—is to take responsibility for it. We are responsible for it. No one else. Nobody *makes* us angry; we choose to feel that way. We are not victims of our emotions. We are not helplessly overwhelmed by anger and its emotional relatives (guilt, shame, fear, and frustration). So let's take a hard look at how to manage and control our anger rather than letting it control us.

Changing Anger's Course

If anger is a choice, then we can choose to respond in ways that help discourage rather than encourage it. We have the ability to change course by what we say, how we say it, and when we say it.

Let's look at some conversations that illustrate choices we can make to cause anger to shrivel up and fade away.

Ken, as he often does, walks in late one evening.

"You're late!" Wendy says, and it isn't for the sake of passing on information. It's a verbal shot across the bow.

"I know how to tell time," Ken replies. "I couldn't help it."

"That might work once or twice. But every time? I'd think you could 'help it' once in a while."

"Could you just get off my back, Wendy? It's been a busy day."

"Too busy to call?"

"Too busy to have to check in with my 'babysitter.'"

"Ken, don't be such a jerk."

"Me? Why don't you stop being such a nag?"

Wendy suddenly realizes she can choose to break this pattern. "Hey, let's stop this. I'm sorry. What's really bugging you? What happened? Are you all right?"

Ken can then choose for or against anger. If he chooses to remain in his anger, he might say, "Nothing happened. I'm just tired of *you* hounding me." But if he chooses to let go of the anger cycle, he might respond, "Yeah, I'm sorry too. I just had a bad day at work. It's not you."

Here's another example:

A coworker tells you in a demeaning tone of voice, "You look awful. I don't suppose you'll be much help at the meeting this afternoon. I wish *I* had time to party every night."

Exhausted and stressed, and with little patience or tolerance, you reply sarcastically, "Oh yeah, that was it. A party. Good thing *you* weren't invited."

Your coworker backs off but begins to tell others negative things about you.

Let's replay this last interaction, making a few changes.

A coworker looks at you and says, "You look awful. What happened?"

You reply, "The kids are sick, and I was up most of the night."

We have the power with our words, intonations, and actions to *incite and ignite* anger or *diffuse and deter* it. When others are rude and inconsiderate, we can respond in ways that dissipate rather than escalate the anger. It's our choice.

Dealing with Angry People

Again, when you find yourself in a situation with an angry person, you have a choice to make. Do you stay and try to work things out, or is it best to leave the situation or take a time-out? When someone is yelling, it's easy to jump on the anger bandwagon. The first thing you can do is ask God for wisdom to direct you. Should you stay or leave? Should you listen or push toward a resolution? Should you be a punching bag or stand up for what you believe? Should you try to help the person or try to get the person help? Or perhaps realize this is not your battle or responsibility?

Consider Options before Getting Angry

When Joe came to counseling one week, this thirty-eight-year-old businessman was obviously mad. He wasted no time telling me (Becca) what his wife had done a few days earlier. "I asked her to pick something up at the store that I really needed, and she forgot. I had specifically told her that it was important to me. It's like she doesn't even care about me anymore. When I'm out of sight, I'm out of mind. At times I feel like we're just coexisting." As he began to wind down, I asked how each of them responded—whether remorsefully, apologetically, defensively, and/or negatively. I then asked if there were any other possible ways to evaluate her forgetfulness. Was she feeling overwhelmed? Was she experiencing PMS? Had she gotten bad or sad news that day? Was she often absentminded? And so on.

After identifying other possibilities, I asked him to figure out what his response would have been if he'd known she'd just received word that something she'd hoped for hadn't come through, or if she wasn't feeling well, or if she was feeling stretched and pulled in all directions. We even discussed other possible emotional responses if his evaluation was, in fact, correct—that she didn't care about him or his needs. At the end of the session, he said, "You made me work hard today, but I learned that I can evaluate things in more than one way, and that I have a choice about how I respond."

> I learned that I can evaluate things in more than one way, and that I have a choice about how I respond.

We all need to learn that we have choices in how we evaluate, feel, and behave. Our emotional response to an event is determined by our evaluation of that event. For example, if a car cuts me off, I can evaluate the situation in several ways, each leading to different emotional responses. If I think the person must be having an emergency and needs to get somewhere fast, then my emotional response might be compassion. If I think the person is an irresponsible jerk, my emotional response would be different—anger or perhaps pity.

Unfortunately, we usually encounter situations so quickly that we don't have much time to evaluate and choose a response. We react out of instinctual reflexes. Our responses are innate or well ingrained—and frequently anger is what jumps out. That's why many of our emotional responses need to be reprogrammed. Though it's hard and it takes time, we encourage you to begin the process of reevaluating anger-producing situations. Our instinctual evaluation can be like a roulette wheel—we don't know where it will land. We need to train our hearts and minds to evaluate in ways that honor God. We need to run our responses through the test that asks if they are appropriate or inappropriate, acceptable or unacceptable, godly or sinful.

Here's how it works: An event leads to an evaluation. That evaluation then leads to both an emotional and a behavioral response. The goal of our evaluation is to find or identify the best and wisest response.

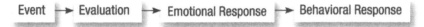

Event ▶ Evaluation ▶ Emotional Response ▶ Behavioral Response

Effective Evaluation

The key task, then, is evaluation. This is where the work is done. When something happens, the emotion we feel is dependent on our assessment of what happened. We ask ourselves: Are there other ways to evaluate what happened? What might be happening with the other person? Am I taking the situation too personally? What's going on? What has contributed to my seeing this the way I do? Can/should I change my evaluation?

Let's look at some examples. If my child misbehaves and I evaluate the behavior as deliberate disrespect and disobedience, then I might respond with anger and act with punishment. If I were to evaluate the behavior differently, that the child is unhappy and wants my attention, then my emotional response might be compassion, not anger. I would act on that emotion by spending more time with the child. I would take the opportunity to correct the child's inappropriate response and help him or her find a better form of expression, but I would still address the underlying need. Here's a chart summarizing several scenarios.

Event	Possible Evaluations	Emotional Response	Behavioral Response
A child misbehaves	He or she is being deliberately disrespectful.	Anger	Discipline
	He or she is unhappy and wants attention.	Compassion	Spend time with the child
A friend breaks a date	He or she is irresponsible.	Anger	Seek revenge
	I'm unlikable.	Anger turned toward oneself	Self-punishment, depression
	Gee, that's too bad, but now I am free to do other things.	Happiness	Go have fun
A store is out of item you wanted	I needed that item *now!*	Anger	Malign and boycott the store
	I guess I'll have to go to that other store across town.	Annoyance	Drive to the other store
	I guess I'll have to do without.	Annoyance	Adapt without the item
Your boss says you forgot something in a report	I'm incompetent.	Fear, anger	Avoidance, revenge
	Thanks for letting me know.	Appreciation	Rework the report
	Please recheck; I know I did it.	Confidence	Review the report with your boss
A friend gossips about you	That's rotten!	Anger	Revenge
	They're insecure.	Pity	Reach out

Event	Possible Evaluations	Emotional Response	Behavioral Response
A family member blames you	They're wrong!	Anger	Defensiveness and revenge
	They're right.	Remorse and confession	Change
	They're to blame, not me!	Anger	Revenge
	They're to blame, but it's too painful to admit.	Compassion	Reach out

Our evaluations can and do go awry when we mislabel, over-generalize, stereotype, assume, expect, minimize, catastrophize, and project. Our evaluations are affected by cultural norms, our past experiences, our models, and our own biases, moods, perceptions, beliefs, and values. As we get better at developing alternative interpretations of others' statements, we are less susceptible to unwarranted anger.

What can we do to become better evaluators? We need to learn to take our time and think before we act, being careful not to jump to wrong conclusions. In fact, Jesus's own half brother James wrote to fellow strugglers in the first century about the need to wisely evaluate by controlling their tongues and emotions: "Everyone should be quick to listen, slow to speak and slow to become angry, for man's anger does not bring about the righteous life that God desires" (James 1:19–20). We'll look at this verse more closely in chapters to come, but here let me (Chip) say it has been a great help to me to memorize this verse as a way to "check" my impulsive nature. My unrighteous anger never accomplishes God's purposes and ends up hurting myself and others. In summary, we all need

> My unrighteous anger never accomplishes God's purposes and ends up hurting myself and others.

to seek an objective outside perspective and be open to other possible interpretations or responses to an event.

A Pledge

The support group organization Men Overcoming Abusive Behavior (MOAB) has a pledge that members recite at the beginning and end of each meeting. These statements represent their choices and commitment to change. Some of the key phrases make promises we could all adapt for our daily lives:

I will not do violence.
I will not touch anyone in anger.
I will be nonintimidating.
I will not do violence to property or pets.
I will do one good thing for myself.

Making Changes

If anger is a choice, we may need to make some changes in how we react to people and evaluate events. We need to make wise, healthy, godly choices. We begin with the desire to change. If you don't have it, ask God to plant that it in your heart. We then make a conscious, personal decision to change our anger responses. For change to last, we need to develop a detailed plan of what we want to change and how we plan to do it. Lastly, we must commit to do it with determination. We pledge to keep hanging in there, to not give up when the going gets rough and tough, and to try, try again—with God's help.

The Bottom Line

Whether we let our anger out in aggressive or assertive ways is a choice. When we choose to ponder, meditate, contemplate, and commit ourselves to well-chosen, premeditated words, we can trust God to step in and help us, guide us, and empower us to handle anger his way. It may not be easy—developing new patterns never is—but he is more than willing to meet us where we are and help us get to where we need to be.

Questions to Consider

1. What did you learn in this chapter about how to redirect anger and change its course?
2. Why do you think we are so quick sometimes to assume the worst of other people's motives?
3. Where do you struggle most in your evaluations? Do you tend to mislabel, overgeneralize, stereotype, assume, expect, or minimize? What one specific step could you take to develop healthier evaluations?

Action Steps to Take

- Think about a recent argument. Try to remember what was said and how it was communicated. Then write out a dialogue based on how you think the conversation should have gone if anger had been dealt with appropriately. Focus especially on giving the revised episode an empathetic tone.
- Think about a recent situation that brought your anger to the surface. Mentally walk yourself through alternative evaluations of the other person's words and/or actions that could have changed your perception and reduced or

eliminated your anger. This practice of slowing yourself down and thinking through other possible interpretations of what angered you will establish mental habits that you can use in future situations.

- Implement the suggestions in the paragraph under the subhead "Making Changes."
  1. If your desire to change isn't as strong as you think it should be, ask God to give you that desire.
  2. Make a firm decision to change your anger responses. Writing out a statement declaring this decision and then signing it will help you stick with it.
  3. On paper, develop a detailed plan of how you want to change and how to do it.
  4. Share with a trusted friend your determination to follow through. You may find it helpful to display the written statement from step 2 in a prominent place.

PART 5

GOD'S ANGER MANAGEMENT PLAN

14

Step 1:
Be Quick to Hear

God created man with two ears and one mouth so
that he would listen twice as much as he speaks.

—Chinese Proverb

I magine a wild stallion—a beautiful, strong horse. Then imagine an experienced cowboy mounting it. The horse bucks and twists and has the potential to destroy the cowboy with its power and strength. But with patience, perseverance, and practice, the cowboy carefully continues. After a few days there's a saddle and bridle on the horse, because this beautiful and powerful beast has been tamed. It's still a strong and dangerous animal, but now its power is harnessed and used for good.

Anger is a wild stallion. It needs to be tamed and harnessed for good. It's an emotion full of energy, power, and strength. Though it has the potential to be very destructive, it also has great potential for good. If left unbridled, anger can destroy us and those around us. We need to know how to bring it under control rather than let it control us. If we don't, it can build barriers and turn tourniquets around our heart and mind. Until we learn to use our temper as God intended, anger will always be a problem in our lives. We need to harness it, to understand it, and to understand what God says about it. It isn't evil. It just needs to be tamed.

> **If left unbridled, anger can destroy us and those around us.**

How do we move beyond getting mad, getting even, and getting depressed? How do we learn to allow the Spirit of God to direct our lives so that anger works as God designed it? What practical advice do we need to overcome the destructive parts of anger in our lives? How do we harness the positive power of anger and bridle the negative nagging? How do we tame the stallion?

God's Anger Management Plan

The book of James in the New Testament was written to people who were experiencing hard times. James knew they would be likely to say and do regretful things. In the midst of his encouragement, God inspired him to write a three-part anger management plan. It's simple yet challenging: Be (1) quick to hear; (2) slow to speak; and (3) slow to anger (James 1:19). This plan, written many years ago, hits a bull's-eye for us today. God knows very well that all of us are prone to do and say sinful, stupid, and silly things when stressed. When under pressure, like those first-century Christians, we become easily angered.

But it doesn't end there. We're told in the following verse why we should follow this plan: "for man's anger does not bring about the righteous life that God desires" (James 1:20). If we continue to let anger run wild, we'll never achieve the lifestyle God knows is best for us. It gets in the way and blocks our path, and our lives turn in the wrong direction.

In my (Becca's) professional studies and experience as a psychologist, I have discovered that most anger management techniques and materials seem to fall into these three foundational areas set forth by God long ago:

1. we need to be active and attentive listeners;
2. we need to think before we open our mouths; and
3. we need to slow down our response.

God's advice is timeless. He knows our human tendencies and imperfections and offers us invaluable and practical help.

What does it look like to tame our temper in our lives, in our homes, in our workplaces, and in our cars? In the next few chapters, we'll examine God's anger management plan, looking more closely at each of the commands and providing some practical, helpful tools you can use beginning today. The first challenge is to "be quick to hear."

> **God's advice is timeless. He knows our human tendencies and imperfections and offers us invaluable and practical help.**

Step 1: Be Quick to Hear

The phrase in its original language means to be eager to listen, to be open. It means being ready, available, and desiring to learn. The word translated "hear" means to understand or to grasp. Whenever Scripture encourages us to hear, it's also challenging us to obey. James is saying that in our anger, our immediate response to God, to others, and to our circumstances should be to listen—to be receptive listeners, not reactionary responders. We are to be eager and ready, open and available to try to understand and grasp what is being said. This runs contrary to our instincts. When we're hurt, frustrated, or wounded, we tend to be more reactionary than reflective. We don't stop to listen to others, to the root feelings underlying our anger, or to God. Instead, we let anger take us for a bucking bronco ride. James says the only way to bridle anger is to stop reacting and to be receptive to hearing God's truth. He's encouraging us to develop an attitude of wanting to hear and apply what he says, even when emotions are heating up.

Listening Isn't Easy

When mad, our ability to listen goes downhill fast because we get caught up in our own hurt, frustrations, or insecurity. It helps to remember that *as feelings of anger increase, listening skills decrease.* It's hard to listen when our heart is bleeding and our mind is racing.

Being a good listener isn't easy, even in the course of ordinary life. But it becomes monumentally hard in the midst of conflict. Because of this, we need to work even harder at it.

Learning to be "quick to hear" should be a lifelong goal. It takes effort and energy, strength and stamina. It requires an earnest desire and a steadfast willingness. We need God's help.

A Desire to Learn to Listen

A woman sent Chip the following letter: "I have a real problem with anger—I explode. I have a teenage son, and it seems like we're at it all the time. I feel guilty, and I feel terrible. After hearing you talk about anger, I want you to know that I'm learning to be quick to hear. I'm learning to address the issue of anger." After her letter, she included a copy of the letter she had written to her son.

Dear Tom,

I first want to tell you that I love you very much. I know I get angry with you and I yell a lot. But I want you to know that

that's not the desire of my heart. The truth of the matter is that I've been praying for the knowledge and power to overcome this problem that I have with anger, and lo and behold, God is always faithful. The topic for the sermons at church right now are anger and rage. The pastor is doing his best to teach us how to overcome this angry feeling. Our best instructor is the Lord Jesus. And our best weapon is prayer. Please pray for me to be a better mom and not to get angry. And that I won't sin by hurting you with my words. I love you and I'm very proud of you.

Love,
Mom

This woman is learning what it means to be quick to hear. She wants to "hear" what's really going on underneath her anger, to hear her son's needs better, and to hear what God says about anger. That's a great place to start!

What Are We Supposed to Hear?

The first question to ask is, "What am I supposed to hear?" We believe there are three areas that require a good listening ear:

1. Learn to listen to your heart to understand the root feeling fueling your anger.
2. Learn to listen to what others are saying by developing good listening skills.
3. Learn to listen to God's voice and what he desires for you, even in the midst of emotionally charged situations.

HEAR THE PRIMARY EMOTION OR ROOT REASON FOR OUR ANGER

Becoming quick to hear is remembering to ask ourselves the key question: "What is the anger telling me?" We can learn to listen to anger long enough to hear what's beneath it. We learn not to entertain and obsess about the angry thoughts but seek to identify the primary emotion. Remember, anger is that light on the dashboard of your soul that says there's a problem under the hood. Listen to your heart and hear what's really going on. Are you feeling jealous, hurt, misunderstood, embarrassed, guilty, afraid, insecure, sad, or trapped? Are you feeling hurt from an unmet need? Is it frustration from an unfulfilled expectation? Is it insecurity from feeling threatened? Being "quick to hear" is listening to your heart and uncovering the root reason for the anger.

Hear Others

At numerous White House receptions, Franklin D. Roosevelt would flash a big smile and greet the many guests. One evening he decided to find out whether anybody was really listening to what he was saying. As each person came up to him with extended hand, he said, "I murdered my grandmother this morning." People would automatically respond with comments such as, "How lovely!" or "Just keep up the good work!" Nobody listened to what he was saying, except for one foreign diplomat. When the president said, "I murdered my grandmother this morning," the diplomat responded, "I'm sure she had it coming."

Studies have shown that we spend as much as 80 percent of waking hours communicating. Of this, we spend approximately 45 percent listening. In spite of such a significant investment of our time, this important skill is rarely taught. Our schools focus primarily on the three Rs—reading, 'riting, and 'rithmetic. In fact, educational programs spend much more time teaching reading and writing, the lesser used communication skills, than on listening and speaking, the most commonly used communication skills.

Better listening skills would resolve a lot of conflicts before they happen. Our anger is often a reaction to someone's critical or confusing words, but we can lessen the number of times anger is triggered. How? As we become better listeners, we often discover that some of our anger is simply due to miscommunication, misunderstanding, or someone using words that to us are laden with emotion.

Listening is an art that must be cultivated. It is not an inherent ability acquired at birth but a skill to be developed with determination. It takes a conscious effort, because hearing and listening are not synonymous. One may have heard what was said but may not have

> **Listening is an art that must be cultivated.**

listened. Jesus was often quoted as saying, "He who has ears, let him hear." He admonished the multitudes to listen not just with their ears, but with their hearts and minds also.

Listening is an essential ingredient in anger management. We need to hear not only the words others say but, more importantly, the feelings behind their words. We lessen our anger-response when we hear others' heart and hurts. As we listen beyond the words spoken, we cultivate a better understanding of what fuels their words and deeds. One of the greatest deterrents to an angry reaction is empathy. When we willfully seek to understand where the other person is coming from and why they feel the way they feel, it changes how we react.

> **When we willfully seek to understand where the other person is coming from and why they feel the way they feel, it changes how we react.**

Though we may sharply disagree with what someone is saying, we become less easily angered as we become more tolerant, gracious, and understanding—both of others and of our own frailties.

Being a Good Listener

Listening doesn't come easy for many of us. Perhaps you are an incessant talker, easily distractible, or find it hard to concentrate when others talk. Perhaps you find many people and situations boring or are literal-minded and find it difficult to understand what emotions may lie beneath someone's words. Whoever you are, whatever your strengths and weaknesses, here are some helpful and practical suggestions on being a good listener:

1. Stop talking. (When we're talking, we aren't able to listen and to understand another's perspective.)
2. Minimize distractions as much as possible. (It's hard to listen when the television, radio, phone, computer, or stereo are on, or with a newspaper in our hand.)
3. Concentrate and give your undivided attention. Listening is hard work and requires discipline.
4. Utilize your thought speed to focus on what's being said. Because you think faster than the other person talks, it's easy to daydream and forget to concentrate on listening. Utilize your mental thought processes in concentrating on what the person is saying and/or trying to say rather than on your next (defensive) response.
5. Maintain eye contact. It enhances your listening skills and lets the other person know you're listening.
6. Listen for what is *not* being said. Be aware of the feelings behind the words. Look for clues in their behavior and other nonverbal cues. Try to understand what they are thinking and feeling.
7. Don't interrupt. Occasional words of affirmation assure the person that you are listening, but they shouldn't divert the conversation.
8. Try not to lose concentration if the person uses emotionally laden words. (We often get distracted and lose concentration if the person uses cuss words or words that we feel are "fighting words.")

9. Don't be quick to judge a person or conversation as uninteresting or "silly." Don't tune out before adequately tuning in.
10. Ask clarifying questions, if needed, in order to more fully understand what the other person is saying. It's better to ask questions than to simply assume you understood what someone said.

Our goal is to become active, attentive, empathetic listeners. So choose two or three of the above listening skills and give them a try at home or on the job. See if becoming a better listener doesn't lower your anger quotient.

Hearing God

Finally, but perhaps most importantly, we should always seek to be quick to hear God and his desires for us. Not long ago, I (Becca) was angry about not being asked to do something I really wanted to do. I was disappointed, and my disappointment turned into anger. As my mind searched for defensive accusations to hurl at those in charge, I sensed that I should pray. Though that isn't always the first thing to come to mind when we're angry, it's always appropriate—whether we feel like it or not. And as I prayed, God seemed to say loud and clear, "This is *my* will. Trust me." My anger began to wash away as I gained God's perspective. This happened because I stopped to listen.

How do we hear God? We hear him and allow him to speak as we read his Word. Often as we read, we discover new insights, find direction, or are struck by a verse that's especially applicable to us and our current situation. We can also hear God as we pray and allow the Holy Spirit to bring thoughts into our hearts and minds. We may seek

> **Hearing God slows down our anger response.**

godly counsel, asking a spiritually mature, objective individual to help us sort out what concerns us. As we hear from the Creator of our souls, our perspective begins to change, sometimes dramatically. Hearing God slows down our anger response.

The Bottom Line

If we want to tame the anger stallion, we first need to be "quick to hear." This means that we are:

- Quick to hear what's fueling our anger
- Quick to hear others (to be active, attentive listeners)
- Quick (ready) to hear God (to listen to what God has to say)

Questions to Consider

1. How much intentional effort did you put into becoming a good listener and oral communicator when you were growing up? Did you work on those skills, or did you, like most people, simply develop them unconsciously?
2. What are the top two or three distractions that keep you from being a good listener?
3. Who is the hardest person for you to listen to? Why?

Action Steps to Take

- Review the ten suggestions for being a good listener. Put a (+) by the ones you're best at and a (–) by the ones you need to improve on.
- Think about a person, place, or thing at which you feel angry. Mentally walk yourself through the three listening areas:

166

1. Hear what is fueling your anger. What's underneath it?
2. Hear others. What do you think they were thinking or feeling?
3. Hear God. How does God want you to deal with it? What does he want you to do?

- Choose one conversation each day this week in which to practice your listening skills, regardless of whether that conversation has any potential for conflict or not. Practice focusing, making eye contact, noticing feelings behind the words, etc., until these efforts become a habit for you.

15

Step 2:
Be Slow to Speak

He who talks much cannot talk well.

—Carlo Goldoni

It often shows a fine command of language to say
nothing.

—Anonymous

It began as a pleasant dinner conversation, but it turned sour
before the appetizers were finished. Five of the six guests knew
each other well, but the sixth was a newcomer. And when he
heard a flippant comment about a serious social issue—which
apparently had become the focus of his personal mission in life
and the subject of his most passionate feelings—he went off on
a diatribe that rebuked the commentator's flippancy and drasti-
cally dampened the mood for the rest of the evening.

As it turns out, the group really saw eye to eye on that serious
social issue, and the flippant comment was a feeble attempt to

mock those on the "wrong" side of the argument. If the newcomer had known his conversation partners better—and if he had asked a simple question or two, such as, "Do you really mean that?" or "Where do you really stand on that issue?" he would have discovered that he was among like-minded friends who were simply used to joking with each other in an offbeat manner. His diatribe could have been avoided, and the evening could have actually been fun. Instead, he left the restaurant that night wondering if his would-be friends considered him a humorless stick-in-the-mud and if he would ever be invited to dinner again.

Many of us can relate to that story, either as the one expressing anger too quickly or as someone on the receiving end of it. The frustrating thing about those situations is that they can be easily avoided with a slightly slower "response mechanism." A few polite questions, a mental balance sheet weighing the costs and benefits of picking a certain battle, and a simple ability to wait a couple of minutes can usually prevent misunderstandings and keep relationships at an enjoyable level. The problem is that many of us haven't been trained to use such helpful tools—or are not even aware of them.

In chapter 14, we began looking at God's anger management plan—his strategy to help us so that anger doesn't run wild. It's a simple yet challenging process. Be (1) quick to hear; (2) slow to speak; and (3) slow to anger. Let's now look at the second piece of godly advice—being slow to speak—and continue to learn the basics of temper training.

Step 2: Be Slow to Speak

For most of us, the times we wish we hadn't said something far outnumber the times we wish we had. We regret our words far more than we regret our silences. Being slow to speak means that we think before we speak, that we weigh our words carefully. As is often said, "The average man thinks about what he has said; the above average about what he is going to say."

Being slow to speak doesn't mean that we talk slowly, as if we're in slow motion. It means that we watch our words and silence our tongues. The literal meaning of this phrase in the original Greek text is to stop, meditate, or ponder before we let something come out of our mouths. It means to prohibit or restrain ourselves from words we might later regret, to contemplate and to reflect upon what we want to communicate. Rather than speaking out of anger or impulse, we are to stop and think.

> The average man thinks about what he has said; the above average about what he is going to say.

If we silence our speech, at least for a moment, we keep harsh, critical, wounding words from piercing others' hearts. As Proverbs tells us, "He who holds his tongue is wise. He who guards his lips guards his life, but he who speaks rashly will come to ruin" (Prov. 13:3). "Do you see a man who speaks in haste? There is more hope for a fool than for him" (Prov. 29:20). It's foolish to speak in haste. We must weigh our words before using them. Our goal is to think before we speak, to reflect rather than react. If we don't, we run the risk of saying and doing things that are not completely true. We may tell white lies; we may say others agree with us when they don't; we may slander with malicious intent.

Although we often don't take our words very seriously, God has some very strong things to say about what comes out of our mouths. Until we begin to get his perspective on our speech, we will continue to reap the negative consequences of our unrestrained words. I challenge you to read through the following verses slowly and purposefully and ask God to help you begin taking your speech as seriously as he does.

> I will watch my ways and keep my tongue from sin; I will put a muzzle on my mouth. (Ps. 39:1)

A man of understanding holds his tongue. (Prov. 11:12)

He who guards his mouth and his tongue keeps himself from calamity. (Prov. 21:23)

Keep your tongue from evil and your lips from speaking lies. (Ps. 34:13)

Even a fool is thought wise if he keeps silent, and discerning if he holds his tongue. (Prov. 17:28)

Reckless words pierce like a sword, but the tongue of the wise brings healing. (Prov. 12:18)

The tongue has the power of life and death. (Prov. 18:21)

According to these verses, our reckless words can bring calamity, lies, evil, and even emotional death. Our bridled tongue brings understanding, wisdom, healing, and life.

Can you remember when someone has unleashed their tongue on you? Or what about when you let loose and let it rip? Were any of those relationships damaged? Are some still injured or awkward? Thinking about those times may give us the motivation to keep our mouths shut.

"Sharp words usually end up cutting our own throat," someone has said. What can you do to get your minds in gear before your tongue is unleashed?

Controlling Anger's Verbal Flood

Many people truly believe they can't control their anger. "It just boils up. I don't even think. It just comes out of my mouth." Perhaps you grew up in a feuding family where shouting matches were a daily occurrence. You may think that since it has been modeled for you all those years, it's too ingrained and untam-

171

able. Don't hide behind that lie! You can change! Anger is not inherited. It's a choice.

What do you do when your car overheats? You stop and let it cool down. This first step is to take a break from the heated situation and buy yourself some time. Why? To figure out what you're really feeling and to avoid saying something you'd regret. As we've discussed, when you begin to feel anger brewing, stop and ask, "What's going on? What am I feeling?"

> **Anger is not inherited. It's a choice.**

Take a Time-out

Before God redirected me (Chip) to become a pastor, I was a school teacher and basketball coach. I loved playing hoops and equally enjoyed coaching it. When the intensity of a game was at its peak, and the crowd and momentum began to favor the other team, I learned quickly that you have to call a time-out. In fact, as you study great coaches and championship teams, you realize that the difference between winning and losing is often knowing when to call one. Whether you signal with your hands or yell it out loud, you make sure the referee knows that you want to interrupt the intensity and take a break.

Likewise, if you feel anger beginning to burn inside, stop and cool down. Taking a time-out will help you and others feel safer and in more control. It doesn't matter if you're in the middle of a heated discussion. You know that if you don't cool down, you'll lose your cool. So stop and get away from the person or situation. Go for a walk, write in a journal, take a bath, go for a run, punch a pillow, or close your eyes and pray—do whatever it takes to help you calm down and sort out your feelings. Use the Anger ABCDs to help you figure out what you're feeling and why. If and when you return to the situation or pick up the conversation again, you'll have a better understanding of what was lying underneath it.

MOAB (Men Overcoming Abusive Behavior), like most anger management programs, encourages participants to use time-outs when they feel anger increasing. They use, among other things, a time-out contract aimed at helping participants commit to healthier responses.

A time-out is

> when you physically remove yourself from the setting, leaving before a verbal or physical altercation, not after something hurtful has happened. Rather than "losing it," individuals who take appropriate time-outs establish to themselves that they can indeed control their anger enough to get out of trouble. There are many tactics angry individuals can take during their time-outs that will help them calm themselves. A time-out can be viewed as a responsible action that prevents irresponsible ones.[1]

During the time-out, it's important to engage in activities or talk with people who do not cause your anger to escalate. Your goal is to calm down, to clarify your concerns, and to begin to see the issue from the other person's perspective. "Individuals who take time-outs must be committed to returning to issues that need to be handled. Otherwise time-outs simply become another manipulative device, something used to avoid the issue. A time-out is taken so that a concern can be addressed rather than getting lost in personal attacks, defensiveness, and rage; it should not be used to evade problems or as a weapon against others."[2]

> A time-out can be viewed as a responsible action that prevents irresponsible ones.

It will be necessary to discuss the time-out tool ahead of time, whether with a mate, roommate, family member, or coworkers. Each person is told to make a time-out gesture (a T with your hands) if they feel either their own anger or the other person's escalating. A previously agreed-upon time frame, such as an hour, then begins. The purpose of this time is not to fume or to build your case, but to have sufficient time to calm down and get perspective on the situation. One of the potential problems here is that some people tend to ignore the concern and never come back to rectify it. The MOAB material states, "When you return, check in with the other person. Find out whether both of you are ready to return to a cooler discussion of the conflict. If so, do so; if not, then set a specific time when both of you will be willing to try again."[3] *The time-out contract encourages resolution, not running away.*

Time-out Contract (MOAB)

When I realize that my (or my partner's) anger is rising, I will give a T signal for a time-out and leave at once. I will not hit or kick anything, and I will not "slam" the door. I will return in no later than one hour. I will take a walk, go to a meeting, use up my anger energy in some constructive way and will not use drugs or alcohol while I am away. I will try not to focus on resentments.

If my partner gives a T signal and leaves, I will return the sign and let my partner go without hassle, no matter what is going on. I will not drink or use drugs while my partner is away, and I will avoid focusing on resentment.

Signed: _____ Date: _____

Signed: _____ Date: _____

In *When Anger Hurts*, the authors warn, "*Do not* say, 'You are making me angry' or 'you're getting out of control.' These kinds of statements will inevitably lead to a defensive posture and escalation rather than the hoped-for cooling off and safety of temporary separation."[4]

Taking a time-out forces us to be "slow to speak" as we take time away from potentially harmful words and actions. Time-outs help us silence our screams and weigh our words.

Creative Time-outs

There are times when walking away isn't possible or preferred—in the car, at work, at a meeting, in a restaurant, or in a store. What can you do in these situations? The author of the *Anger Work-out Book* suggests being creative in developing time-out strategies. The goal is to do something that will prevent an escalation.

Here are some examples of creative time-outs:

- In a car: Listen to three songs on the car radio before you continue your "discussion"; stop to get some gas and get out of your car for a stretch.
- At work: Take a ten-minute break before getting back to the task at hand.
- In a restaurant: Order first, then talk. Go into a bathroom for ten minutes and wash your face, or step outside for five minutes and get a breath of fresh air.

All of these are based on the time-out strategy of interrupting your anger and can be used in confining situations.[5] They are among the many things you can do to slow down your response time so you don't put your foot in your mouth.

> The goal is to do something that will prevent an escalation.

Putting these things into practice will help you tame your anger. Step one is to become a reflective listener instead of reactionary responder. Step two involves buying yourself some time. This will increase your chances of being able to hold your tongue, allow you to process your anger, enable you to evaluate what's going on beneath the surface, and give yourself an opportunity to get under control.

The Bottom Line

"I will watch my ways and keep my tongue from sin; I will put a muzzle on my mouth" (Ps. 39:1). When we feel anger beginning to burn inside, we need to stop and cool down.

Questions to Consider

1. In what situations do you struggle most to hold your tongue?
2. With whom do you most often find yourself in conversation or in a situation in which holding your tongue is a problem?
3. What new insight do you gain concerning God's view of the importance of our words?
4. What specific ideas and tools will help you think before you speak?

Action Steps to Take

- Identify at least one person—someone you relate to on a regular basis—with whom you might need to develop a time-out contract.
- Come up with your ideal time-out contract and write it down.
  1. Review it with whomever you need to—family, friends, roommate, and/or coworkers.
  2. For the purposes of accountability, have these people sign it.

3. Make an effort to implement it, relying on others to help you track your progress. Ask for both constructive criticism and timely affirmation.

- In your conversations this week, count to ten silently and slowly before you respond to any information or comments that seem to provoke you. Suppressing the urge to respond may be very uncomfortable at first, but remind yourself that a response will always be an option—at a later time and in a calmer manner. Then adamantly refuse to react from your immediate urge.

16

Step 3:
Be Slow to Anger

The greatest remedy for anger is delay.
—Seneca

It was a race against the clock. Superspy James Bond had everything going against him—frantic action, enemies breathing down his neck, ammunition miraculously missing him, and the fate of the planet in his hands. The odds against his success were overwhelming, and the stakes were incredibly high. If the clock ticked down to 0:00, life as we know it would be forever altered.

It didn't, of course. Bond always saves the day. But the race against the clock—no matter how often it occurs in movies, whether it's a digital timer or a very long fuse in an old Western—always makes us nervous. That's because it takes an amazing feat by the hero to stop the seemingly inevitable blast. It's never easy to prevent an explosion.

That's also true when we're mad. We must often accomplish amazing feats in order to defuse the time bomb within us. We

178

feel the anger boiling up inside, and we're about to explode. It takes a lot to disarm us. But the longer the countdown, the better our chances. Amazing feats are much more possible when time is on our side.

"A patient man has great understanding, but a quick-tempered man displays folly," Proverbs 14:29 tells us. The quick-tempered among us explode in anger when we don't get our way. We think, "No one's going to block my goal. Get out of my way." Or, "I can't believe that guy got the promotion instead of me. I'll tell you what I'm going to do. I'm going to talk to So-and-So and get a couple of black marks on his record." When this verse refers to patience, it means a "long-fused person." The verse says that this kind of person has understanding. If we aren't patient and understanding, we become quick-tempered and foolish.

In the first step in God's plan (be quick to hear), you responded by being a receptive, attentive listener. The second step (be slow to speak) was more of an intermediate response. You zip your lips in order to buy yourself some time. These two steps are practical tools for reaching the main goal, which is the third step: be slow to anger. This is a life-changing, life-saving step. This is where you disarm the anger bomb. The

> We must often accomplish amazing feats in order to defuse the time bomb within us.

first two steps lengthen the fuse and add time to the clock, but now it's up to you to do that amazing feat of stopping destructive anger before it bursts. Whether you have a moment or a month, the main goal is to disarm the anger before it destroys you and those around you.

I wonder how many divorces started with some small, inconsequential issues that grew into heated, angry arguments. How many friends, churches, and families have been divided or destroyed because the anger bomb was not defused? Listen to the ancient wisdom of Solomon, the world's wisest man, on the topic of anger:

Do not be quickly provoked in your spirit, for anger resides in the lap of fools. (Eccles. 7:9)

A fool gives full vent to his anger, but a wise man keeps himself under control. (Prov. 29:11)

A fool shows his annoyance at once, but a prudent man overlooks an insult. (Prov. 12:16)

Did you catch the common word in each verse? If not, read over them again and see if you can find the word Scripture often associates with those who don't control their anger.

We make a fool of ourselves when the anger bomb goes off. We do foolish things when we don't disarm it in time.

Changing Reaction to Reflection

The word we translate as anger in the New Testament originates from two very different Greek words. One is *thumos*, which means to blow up. This kind of anger is the rash, reactive, impulsive kind. The other word, *orge*, refers to resentful, ruminating feelings. It's the kind of anger we harbor when someone has attacked us or when someone lets us down or hurts us. This is the kind that festers and becomes a cancerous infection that eats us up on the inside. One word refers to the quick, explosive type, the other to the long, lingering type. They are both destructive and harmful. Both are time bombs that will detonate if we don't do something to disarm them.

> Too many of us have given ourselves permission to vent our frustration. We need to revoke that permission.

When James writes "be slow to anger," he's referring to the lingering type of anger, not the explosive kind. He's encouraging us to change our reaction, to slow it down so there's time for reflection. We need to stop, listen, think, and ask ourselves those key questions:

What's going on inside? Am I feeling angry? (A—acknowledge the anger)

What am I really feeling? What's the root reason for the anger? (B—backtrack to the root reason)

Why am I feeling this way? What has happened? (C—consider the cause)

How should I deal with this? What should I do? (D—determine how to deal with the situation)

Six Ways to Slow Down Your Anger

One sure way to slow down our anger is to learn to use effective communication. "In every conflict, you have a task—to communicate your needs, understand the other person's point of view, and work toward solution."[2] Here are some suggestions for accomplishing these tasks:

1. Communicate your needs in a nonaccusatory manner.
2. Try to understand and acknowledge the other person's point of view.
3. Stick to the issue and the facts (don't attack character).
4. Identify possible solutions (negotiate, compromise, cooperate, take turns, etc.).
5. Maintain calm, respect, and objectivity, and remain open to new input and/or ideas.
6. If the discussion becomes heated, consider taking a time-out.

> In every conflict, you have a task—to communicate your needs, understand the other person's point of view, and work toward solution.

Whether you are slow to anger or quick-tempered, whether the detonator is set to two minutes or two years, it still needs to be disarmed. It's important to acknowledge and remember, too, that those who are "slow to anger" may not have necessarily defused their anger bombs, which can explode in the form of ulcers or other physical ailments, or in the form of deep-seated resentments and bitterness. Either way, you experience the destructive power of the anger bomb. In the next two chapters, we'll look at some ways to reset your detonator—not to cover up your emotions and *appear* to be "slow to anger," but to become truly slow to anger outwardly and, more importantly, in the depths of your heart.

The Bottom Line

The longer the time until we potentially explode, the better our chances of accomplishing the amazing feat of diffusing the anger bomb within us.

Questions to Consider

1. Do you have a short or long fuse? Would others call you "quick-tempered"?
2. What are some things you've done to help lengthen your fuse?
3. Why is it so important to learn to identify and deal with your anger in relationships? What's at stake?

Action Steps to Take

- Identify the two techniques in this chapter that would *most* help you become slower to anger. Then choose one person to practice those two techniques with this week. As these become habits, add the other techniques from this chapter one by one to your approach to relationships.

- Talk with a safe, trusted friend or family member and discuss the last time you were really angry with someone else in the last month. Describe to your confidant the things you could have done differently to lengthen your anger fuse. After you've voiced your thoughts, ask for any additional insights or advice he or she might have.

- Block off forty-five minutes this week to reenvision a relationship that has been affected by your anger. Picture the more positive outcomes that might result from implementing your new insights, and then determine to adjust your reactions until those positive outcomes are achieved. (And be patient—relationship changes don't always happen instantly or even quickly.)

PART 6

LEARNING TO STOP ANGER BEFORE IT STARTS

17

Minimize Stress

> May there be peace within your walls
> and security within your citadels.
>
> —Psalm 122:7

One day I (Becca) decided to keep a mental log of all of the times I felt anger. I wanted to know how often I got angry, what I got angry about, and what triggered the anger. I'd encourage you to try this too—the results were surprising and quite humbling. I was shocked at how often angry feelings came to the surface. Prior to consciously counting these episodes, I had mistakenly assumed that anger was only an occasional visitor to my emotional arsenal. I was wrong. Very wrong.

I had to be honest about my feelings of anger, frustration, and infuriation. I felt either flits or fits of anger at not being able to find my favorite socks, running out of milk, the kids taking so long to get ready, the slow driver in front of me, the long wait at the pharmacy, the store closed on Mondays, having to put gas in the car, the high price of gas, the long line and slow service at the store, the kids leaving their clothes on the floor (again), the computer freezing (again) . . . and I was only halfway through the day! Though some of these feelings could be described as fleeting frustrations, far too many were actual anger.

But another humbling lesson came as I realized that most of the day-to-day anger I experienced was about small, insignificant stuff. If we view our emotions as a valuable energy source, then I was expending way too much on anger. I was wasting emotional energy unnecessarily. In theory, I believe that when we get angry, it should be over noble, needed causes, not over petty pursuits. Unfortunately, however, I wasn't living that way. My daily frustrations were fueled by trivial things.

That's how extensively anger can impact our lives. We get mad not only over big things—deep hurts and ongoing pain—but also over little things, like daily inconveniences and momentary frustrations. We're affected by both the small stuff and the deep devastations.

Some of the annoyances we experience are triggered by deeper anger issues, as with a woman who reacted harshly to the store clerk who informed her that they'd run out of the item she wanted. She was angry at the store for not stocking what she needed, primarily because it triggered long-held pain of not having her needs met as a child.

Many of our daily frustrations, however, are not caused by negative past experiences but by our lifestyle and our attitudes. A man might get angry at the slow driver in front of him simply because he's in a hurry to get where he's going, not because his anger is triggered by lingering past hurts. But regardless of whether anger-producing events trigger deep hurts or daily hassles, we need to develop some prevention skills so that our anger is triggered less frequently and the alarm doesn't sound as often.

Minimizing Stress

When I stopped to look at how often I got angry and what I got angry about, it was hard to admit that it happened too much and too often. I then went a step further and took an introspective look at what contributes to my day-to-day anger. The answer was surprisingly simple—stress.

The relationship between stress and anger in my life isn't unusual. The more pressured, burned out, overwhelmed, or busy we are, the more vulnerable we are to anger. The key to lessening the amount of anger we feel lies in our ability to minimize stress, which is caused by a variety of events and circumstances—our jobs, our home, our relationships, our health, our finances, and our families. Even normal daily life can be stressful. *The more stress we are under, the more likely it is that anger will make an appearance.* Our goal is to reduce it.

> The more pressured, burned out, overwhelmed, or busy we are, the more vulnerable we are to anger.

If you long to reduce the stress and anger quotient in your life, let me encourage you to carefully consider the following stress and anger reducers. The following six strategies will have profound effects on your ability to minimize the pressure in your life.

1. Eliminate Hurry

For many of us, anger kicks in when we're in a hurry. We want to get somewhere or do something fast, and something or someone gets in the way. We've decided our course of action, and we don't want anything or anyone to slow us down. Unfortunately, we can't control others. Some clerks are slow, some drivers are slow, and some lines are slow. Some paths take longer, some tasks take longer, some people take longer. And when people, places, and things don't go at our pace, we generally get mad.

Dallas Willard once passed on some wise advice to a friend: "You must ruthlessly eliminate hurry from your life."[1] That hits most of us right between the eyes. We live in a pack-it-all-in, go-for-the-gusto, the-more-the-better, the-bigger-the-better world. We want to *do* it all and *have* it all, and modern technology enables us to *know* about it all. As a result, our lives are often a flurry of rushing here and there, trying to squeeze as much into twenty-four hours as we can.

> **"You must ruthlessly eliminate hurry from your life."**
> **—Dallas Willard**

We desperately need to slow down. Otherwise we become like those of whom Carl Sandburg wrote: "There are people who want to be everywhere at once, and they seem to get nowhere."[2]

When I realized that much of my anger was fueled by my own pace, I determined to work on eliminating hurry from my life. It was hard—much harder than I thought, especially with four young children on a day of endless errands. "Hurry up! Get your shoes on. Hurry up! Get in the car. Hurry up! Stay with me. Hurry up! Let's go! Hurry up! Hurry up! Hurry up!" One of my children finally asked, "Why are we in a hurry?" I stopped and sadly realized that there was no reason, no place we needed to be. I had simply developed a "hurry up" lifestyle and attitude.

There are times, of course, when we have a good reason to hurry. Getting out of the way of an oncoming car is an example that comes to mind. But if we were to take an honest look at our times of hurry, we would probably discover that in many cases our rush was our own fault because we did not manage our time well and had to compensate for not planning ahead.

A number of years ago, my family and I (Chip) attended family camp. It was a wonderful time of fun together. One of the afternoon activities included a carnival followed by a delicious barbecue dinner. There were game booths, relay races, prizes, and contests.

One of the relay races stands out in my mind. Teams were lined up with the task of running to the other side of the field. At that point each person was required to put their head on a baseball bat and spin around ten times before returning as fast as possible to their team. Sound easy? The result of bending over and spinning around was painfully humorous. When my turn came, I ended up like those before me. After spinning round and round, I too began walking at an angle, fell over, got up, and had my body take me where my mind didn't tell it to go. (Normally I flee from activities that make me look and feel like a fool, but I knew my children would enjoy seeing me fall over and look crazy—and they did.) While others laughed with delight, I struggled to get back to where I wanted to go.

Too often our lives are like that game. We keep spinning around until we feel out of control. We try to do too many things in the precious little time we have.

How is your pace of life? Do you feel sometimes like you're spinning your wheels and not getting much of anywhere? Do you feel like you're turning round and round until you're too dizzy to think straight? It seems that our culture sets us up for that. At times we may feel like screaming, "Stop the world and let me get off!"

As in the game, spinning around too much causes us to fall on our faces, go in the wrong direction, and end up in places we didn't really want to go. We make mistakes, hurt important relationships, make poor decisions, do things we shouldn't, and become much more easily angered.

In *When I Relax I Feel Guilty*, Tim Hansel writes,

Our world seems intoxicated with hurry. It seems to be inundated with a hurricane desire to precipitate the future. One of the greatest sins of this age may be hurry. For in our impatient desire to make things happen, we have, inadvertently, overlooked what was really important. Small wonder, then, that we have lost the ability to immerse ourselves in the simple delights of the earth—the wind against our faces, savory aromas in our nostrils, moist grass beneath our feet, a child in our arms.[3]

Eliminating hurry means that we slow down, plan ahead, and enjoy rather than race through life. A German proverb asks the right question: "What is the use of running when we are not on the right road?" Like a hamster on a wheel, we may end up getting nowhere. The following lists give examples of how our lives can be affected by hurry and also how they can be improved without it. You can probably think of many other examples that apply more specifically to you. Though the transition from one category to another is harder than it looks, the results are well worth it.

> Eliminating hurry means that we slow down, plan ahead, and enjoy rather than race through life.

When I'm in a hurry, I don't notice the flowers blooming alongside the roadside.

When I'm in a hurry, there seem to be a lot more irritating drivers on the road.

When I'm in a hurry, I don't strike up friendly conversations with those around me.

When I'm in a hurry, I avoid people, places, and things that take time and energy.

When I'm in a hurry, I pretend not to see the person behind me in line who only has a few items when I have a cart full of groceries.

When I'm in a hurry, my heart pounds, my muscles tense, and my mind races.

When I'm in a hurry, I rush the kids through the day.

When I'm in a hurry, I don't ask people how they are doing.

When I'm in a hurry, my devotional times are a task not a treasure.

When I'm in a hurry, I'm abrupt with people.

When I'm in a hurry, it feels as if life is a race to be run.

When I'm in a hurry, I get angry more easily and more often.

When I'm *not* in a hurry, I enjoy my food more.

When I'm *not* in a hurry, I smile more and feel calmer inside.

When I'm *not* in a hurry, life seems more enjoyable and less stressful.

When I'm *not* in a hurry, I'll ask others about themselves and how they are doing.

When I'm *not* in a hurry, my times in prayer are more meaningful.

When I'm *not* in a hurry, I'm nicer, more thoughtful, and kinder to others.

When I'm *not* in a hurry, I'm more patient, loving, understanding, and tolerant.

When I'm *not* in a hurry, I'm more creative, more spontaneous—happier.

When I'm *not* in a hurry, things don't bother me as much.

When I'm *not* in a hurry, I don't get angry as often.

God encourages us in his Word to rest in who he is and to bring all of our concerns to him. "Be still, and know that I am God" (Ps. 46:10). "Do not be anxious about anything, but in everything, by prayer and petition, with thanksgiving, present your requests to God. And the peace of God, which transcends all understanding, will guard your hearts and your minds in Christ Jesus" (Phil. 4:6–7). The very fact that he tells us these things indicates that (1) it isn't as impossible as we might think it is (quite the opposite, in fact), and (2) he intends to help us if we'll ask him to. The result when we do this can be dramatic. Our inner peace is rooted in him. Try saying this prayer written by Orin Crain:

> Slow me down, Lord.
> Ease the pounding of my heart by the quieting of my
>   mind.
> Steady my hurried pace with a vision of the eternal
>   reach of time.
> Give me, amid the confusion of the day, the calmness of
>   the everlasting hills.
> Break the tensions of my nerves and muscles with the
>   soothing music of the singing streams that live in
>   my memory.
> Teach me the art of taking minute vacations—of slow-
>   ing down to look at a flower, to chat with a friend,
>   to pat a dog, to smile at a child, to read a few lines
>   from a good book.
> Slow me down, Lord, and inspire me to send my roots
>   deep into the soil of life's enduring values, that I
>   may grow toward my greater destiny.
> Remind me each day that the race is not always to the
>   swift; that there is more to life than increasing its
>   speed.
> Let me look upward to the towering oak and know that
>   it grew great and strong because it grew slowly
>   and well.[4]

This poetic prayer not only encourages us to slow down, it points out some sure signs that we need to do so—a pounding heart and tension in nerves and muscles. Our body often sends us stress messages, but we frequently ignore them. Increased headaches, muscle strain, and stomach problems, among other symptoms, announce the presence of stress and our need to slow down.

What do you need to do to slow down, to keep your life from feeling like it is spinning "out of control"? If you aren't sure yet how you can reduce the hurry in your life, the remaining steps will help you.

2. Downsize Expectations

In graduate school, I (Becca) took a class on administration. One of the things the professor encouraged us to do was to develop daily and weekly to-do lists to assist in goal attainment and organization. But, he also wisely advised us, "Once you've written down your daily to-do list, cut it in half." He knew we attempt to do more than we generally can do in a day. He knew the human tendency to stuff our days too full, to hurry about in a frenzy. He knew we'd feel more successful and good about ourselves when we're able to accomplish what we set out to do. If we set out with unrealistic goals, we run the risk of feeling like a failure when we fall short of them.

When I only have one hour before a meeting and I still have five things to do, I'm setting myself up for failure, frustration, and anger. That's when I need to revise my to-do list and downsize my expectations.

Some of us struggle with trusting others enough to delegate tasks, so we end up doing things ourselves. In this case, it's not so much that others are too demanding. It's just that we're unable to let go of items on our list. Then it's time to reevaluate, to loosen control, to delegate, and to trust others more.

Downsizing expectations involves learning to say no. Stress is often created by our inability to set limits. We end up doing things and going places against our will when we answer affirmatively too easily. It's hard to say that simple two-letter word, but we have to learn how.

Why is it hard to say no? As Christians, we've been taught much about servanthood and the need to give to others selflessly, so it can feel wrong to reject a request for our time and energy. We also *want* to please others. Sometimes that's because we want approval and fear rejection. We want others to like us, so we say yes out of our insecurity. But sometimes it's simply because we truly desire to help. We want to be Christlike, and our greatest example literally poured out his life on behalf of others. So that desire is good and godly, but it needs to be balanced. Jesus also went away by himself to rest at times. We don't serve well if we burn out quickly.

Saying no helps keep anger from growing into a raging monster. Sometimes you have to speak up and let a boss, spouse, friend, pastor, or family member know that you don't want to do something they requested. There's nothing wrong with that; in fact, it can help strengthen relationships to set some boundaries in them. "Some people are very demanding. They've learned to be that way because it gets results. [Don't] waste time blaming people for their obnoxious or manipulative styles. You focus instead on how to get across the message that you have limits. It's your responsibility to say no to the things you prefer not to do."[5] God has given you the responsibility of being the steward of your gifts, skills, and schedule. You don't dishonor other people by saying no at appropriate times; you honor God by managing your resources well.

When you learn to say no, you shrink your to-do list and reduce hurry all at the same time. Life's pace slows down because you aren't running around doing additional, unwanted tasks. Your tasks decrease as you do those things you want to and should do, eliminating excess items expected of you by others or that you could and should delegate. You reevaluate your commitments and reexamine your priorities.

Is that hard to do? Absolutely. Many requests are made of you each day. Some you enjoy and do willingly and readily. Others you may not enjoy but should do anyway. But some requests require you to stand up for yourself and say an unwavering no. It's okay to consider your time, energy, commitments, likes, and dislikes. Saying no doesn't mean you are selfish or self-centered. Though you may initially feel some guilt over avoiding some commitments you would normally have accepted, you'll find that you become better able to serve God, your family, your coworkers, and your friends if you limit your responsibilities to those you have time and energy to do well.

Here are some suggestions on how to say no:

1. Give yourself time by saying, "I'll get back to you on that" or "I'd like to think about it first."
2. Don't over-apologize, as it could leave the impression that you feel guilty and could easily be manipulated or talked into doing what the person wants.
3. Don't put yourself down by refusing to do something, saying, "I'm not good at that" or "You should ask someone else who's better at that." The person may respond by trying to convince you that you are able to do what they want.
4. Be specific about what you will and will not do. For example, "I can help with typing but not with writing or editing."[6]
5. Above all, be honest. Don't make excuses or twist the truth just to make you or the other person feel better. Communicate simply and clearly.

3. Admit Your Mistakes

The person who can own up to mistakes is greater than the one who knows how to avoid making them.

In counseling over the years, I (Becca) have encountered numerous people who grew up in homes where blame was tossed around like a hot potato. As I listened to the various stories, it became clear to me that much hurt and harm could be avoided if people were more willing to accept rather than project blame.

Why do we find it so hard to say the simple phrase, "I was wrong"? Why are improprieties ignored, follies forgotten, and indiscretions denied? Why are necessary apologies unnecessarily neglected? Because we don't like admitting our blunders, errors, failures, and sin. To do so is to confront our imperfections, to consider our frailties, and to admit our humanity.

Since the beginning of time, we've been a people who would rather make excuses than accept responsibility. When Adam and Eve ate the forbidden fruit, Eve blamed the serpent, and Adam blamed Eve—and even had the audacity to blame God!

All too often, we would rather defend our mistakes. Much too much energy is spent trying to cover up, deny, minimize, or transfer blame. This can happen in any relationship, but it's especially common in marriages, where defensiveness is allowed to creep in over time. But regardless of the relationship, defensiveness rarely (if ever) accomplishes what we want it to accomplish. Rather than protecting our own dignity, reputation, or sense of wounded pride, it alienates others. Our energy would be better spent simply acknowledging and admitting our errors, which tends to attract others. A lot of unnecessary time is wasted when the whole mess could have ended with, "I'm sorry. I blew it."

> **Much too much energy is spent trying to cover up, deny, minimize, or transfer blame.**

We're more apt to use anger as a weapon when we're defending ourselves and our actions. To fend off intrusions, we put up a blockade that few will attempt to penetrate. It bothers us when others observe, respond to, or bring mistakes to our attention.

In *The Friendship Factor*, author Alan Loy McGinnis states, "Since relationships are the most difficult things we attempt in this life, of course we will make mistakes. And when we do, we can save ourselves a good deal of misery by apologizing."[7] We must make sure, however, that our apologies are more than mere words. Those hard-to-say yet helpful-to-hear words must be accompanied by a genuine desire to discontinue whatever it was that we did wrong. Without a repentant spirit, our apologies are meaningless.

Being willing to admit our imperfections increases our humility and simultaneously decreases our anger. (It also makes us more interesting and enjoyable to be around—and more highly respected.) Someone has said, "Any fool can defend his mistakes (and most do), but the wise man admits his mistakes and refrains from repeating them." One sure way to reduce our anger quotient is to be willing to accept our imperfections and say, "I'm sorry."

4. Laugh More

After I'd leaned over and spun around that bat ten times at the family camp, I couldn't walk straight. As hard as I tried to get back to the other side of the relay line, I couldn't do it. I went in the wrong direction and fell to the ground. The harder I tried, the funnier it became. My children doubled over with laughter.

Why? Because it *is* funny to see a person lose control so much that they can't walk straight. If we were to stop and look at our hectic lives from an outside perspective, we would probably laugh at how frantic a pace we try to live. Our busyness and unrealistic expectations cause us to do some strange, silly, and stupid things. Maybe we need to step back, take an objective look at our lives, see the folly, and let out a big laugh.

Perhaps this is what we *should* do when life seems to be going in the wrong direction and we keep falling down. When we're on the verge of an anger attack, when we begin to feel uptight, when life is spinning out of control, a big laugh—even at ourselves—would really help put things in perspective.

One of the best antidotes for anger is laughter. The more we laugh, the less anger we feel. Proverbs 17:22 reminds us that "a cheerful heart is good medicine, but a crushed spirit dries up the bones." The more serious we are about life, the more effort it takes to see the humorous side of it. The more serious we are about life, the easier it is for anger to express itself. The less we laugh, the more anger we experience. The more we laugh, the less anger we experience. Instead of taking life and ourselves so seriously, we need to be able to laugh at both.

> One of the best antidotes for anger is laughter.

Being able to laugh at life doesn't mean being blind to its difficulties and sorrows. It means that we can rise above them, trusting in our sovereign God. When we get too serious, we lose perspective. At those times we become more easily frustrated, more self-focused, less tolerant, and less patient. Anger is triggered easily.

I had a pleasant surprise one day in counseling. A forty-year-old married woman was sharing her agitation about a situation that had occurred that week. As she vented her anger, her demeanor changed. But unlike most people, the more she spewed her anger, the more she began to smile. She finally stopped, let out a big laugh, and said, "I sure made a mountain out of a molehill. Sometimes I take things too seriously."

Perhaps you've read the letter written by an anonymous person in the latter years of life. Here's part of it:

> If I had my life to live over again . . . I would be sillier than I have been this trip. I know of very few things I would take seriously. I would be crazier.

This is important advice: don't take things too seriously, and let yourself be silly and crazy.

Laughter helps heal anger. It's a warm blanket on a cold soul. It forces anger away and helps us to regain perspective on what's really important in life.

5. Take Care of Yourself

Our anger gauge goes up (along with our stress gauge) when we neglect sleep, exercise, good nutrition, and fun. The more exhausted we are, the more easily angered we become. Poor eating habits drain our precious energy, leaving us weak in body and in spirit. Certain medications and substances can also result in our being more easily agitated at life's ups and downs. Anger management specialists generally require participants to abstain from substance use, knowing that drugs generally lower one's inhibitions about expressing and exploding in anger. The bottom line is that the healthier we are, the better we feel about ourselves and life. And the better we feel about ourselves, the less stress and anger we experience.

6. Know What Triggers Your Anger

Each of us is unique. Our personalities and past experiences shape us differently. Because of this, we each respond to anger in different ways. What angers me may not upset you. What ticks you off may not even bother me. While most of us would feel anger when someone is rude, we may not respond to the same degree.

Introverts are more easily angered at continual interruptions than extroverts are. A sports fan will get mad at a referee's bad call that wouldn't even phase a non–sports fan. A pet owner would be furious at the mistreatment of animals more easily than a non–pet owner would. I get angry at violations of my personal space much more than my friend does. A client experiences more anger at bad drivers than I do.

It is helpful, then, to identify anger-producing people, places, and things in your life. If you can foresee those things that provoke you, then you can attempt to avoid, eliminate, or minimize them. Though many situations are unpredictable and unavoidable, identifying potential anger producers ahead of time gives you the chance to short-circuit them. Identify how you might feel and what would be appropriate, healthy, godly responses.

By identifying anger triggers, we decrease their severity and intensity, because we increase our ability to develop and plan for healthy responses.

The Bottom Line

Much of the anger we feel is directly related to the amount of stress we experience. The more pressured, stressed out, burned out, overwhelmed, or busy we are, the more vulnerable we are to anger. But identifying those people, places, and things that normally trigger stress, we can proactively manage the pressure we feel and free ourselves to function in a healthy and wholesome way without being overburdened.

Anger Reduction Lifestyle (Anger Prevention), Part 1

Minimize Stress
1. Eliminate hurry.
2. Downsize expectations.
3. Learn to say no.
3. Admit mistakes and imperfections.
4. Laugh more—don't take life or yourself too seriously.
5. Take care of yourself.
6. Know what triggers your anger.

Questions to Consider

1. Do you find yourself getting stressed out and angry over small stuff?
2. Do you feel like your life is sometimes spinning out of control? Do you rush through life? What steps can you take to slow down?

3. What responsibilities do you have right now that you wish you had said no to? What guidelines and criteria can you develop that will help you know when to say no to those kinds of things?

Action Steps to Take

- Complete the following series of questions about admitting mistakes:

Do I readily admit mistakes?	Yes	No	Sometimes
Do I tend to make excuses rather than admit a blunder?	Yes	No	Sometimes
Are my apologies sincere?	Yes	No	Sometimes
Are my apologies accompanied by a genuine attempt to change?	Yes	No	Sometimes
Do I let pride get in the way?	Yes	No	Sometimes
Do I tend to blame others when errors occur?	Yes	No	Sometimes
Were words of apology spoken in the home where I grew up?	Yes	No	Sometimes

- Keep a log of all the times you experience anger.
  1. Analyze and categorize whether the anger producers are big or small.
  2. Identify ways that you can minimize your stress (anger) level over those small things.
- Try to go a day without feeling rushed or hurried. Make a list of what you discover, see, or feel.
- Choose one of the following ways to introduce more laughter into your life this week. (1) Rent a comedy to watch or (2) relive some old stories with family or friends. At the end of the week, take note of whether your level of stress has decreased as a result.

18

Maximize God

With God in our hearts there is little room for anything else.

John lay in his hospital bed, his body throbbing from his recent surgery. Only minutes earlier, he felt fine—or at least he *thought* he felt fine, as he laughed with his friends who had come for a visit. Now the friends were gone, and the pain was almost unbearable.

Down the hall, Sarah had been wallowing in self-pity over the horrible timing of her accident, which had sidelined her from one of the more exciting projects her office had seen in years. But her pity quickly turned from self toward her new roommate—a young mother recently diagnosed with terminal cancer. Her baby was only six months old, and the new mom wasn't expected to see her daughter's first birthday. Suddenly, Sarah's "missed opportunity" didn't look so bad.

Each of these is a story of transformation, not of a situation but of an attitude. John's and Sarah's own circumstances remained the same, but their focus changed. John was distracted from his pain for a moment; Sarah's pity was overshadowed by someone else's condition. By being preoccupied with others, they both lost sight of their own problems.

We can do this with our anger too. We can change our focus. Instead of zeroing in on our hurts, we choose a different perspective. Instead of seeing only pain, we develop empathy toward others. Instead of focusing on the negatives, we open our eyes to the hope and healing around us. It causes us to see

> **The best way to change a perspective is to focus clearly on God.**

things differently. And the best way to change a perspective is to focus clearly on God.

Maximize God

The best way to minimize anger's hold on us is to maximize God's impact and input in our lives. This is the most important step of anger prevention we can ever take. This means that we lean on him, depend on him, spend time with him, and seek him. The more he is a part of our lives, the less destructive unnecessary anger will be.

Let's examine some ways to maximize your relationship with God, ways we believe are essential to reducing anger over deep wounds as well as small irritants.

1. Draw Near to God

In order to maximize God in our lives and to get his healing perspective, we first need to make sure we are in a right relationship with him. The first step is to believe in him as Lord and Savior, acknowledging his rightful role in our lives. God created us specifically for a relationship with him, but throughout the ages, people have chosen to go it alone. They only find that life without him is devoid of meaning and hope.

Getting right with God also means that we lay before him both our sins and our hurts. With regard to our sins, we confess our disobedience and disrespect, our wrong behavior and evil intentions. We repent and receive his gracious forgiveness. With regard to our hurts, we ask him to help us forgive those whom we feel have caused our pain. God commands us to forgive others in response to the formidable, free forgiveness he gives us. Doing so breaks the chain that anger wraps around our soul. (Later we provide a more in-depth look at getting rid of the deep devastation and what we need to do to give God the reins of our life.)

> As we draw near to God, he promises to draw near to us.

As we draw near to God, he promises to draw near to us. As a result, life's deep devastations take on new meaning. We begin to see them from a new perspective. Though he tells us that suffering is inevitable, he also assures us that he can use it to help us grow in godliness.

2. Experience God's Unconditional Love and Acceptance

The LORD is . . . abounding in love. For as high as the heavens are above the earth, so great is his love for those who fear him . . . from everlasting to everlasting the LORD's love is with those who fear him. (Ps. 103:8, 11, 17)

How great is the love the Father has lavished on us, that we should be called children of God! (1 John 3:1)

Get the picture? God loves us. He loves you a lot! And his love is unconditional and everlasting. It's hard for us to fathom the depth of it. It's beyond comprehension. Even in the midst of our sinfulness, pride, self-pity, codependencies, addictions, anger, greed, gossip, dishonesty, jealousy, and more, He still loves us, offering us forgiveness in Jesus's name.

The more we allow God's love to infiltrate every fiber of our being, the less room there is for anger to reside. As we allow his love to course through our veins, anger fades away, and we are empowered to love others. This is the best antidote for anger. I (Becca) love Mother Teresa's response when asked if it made her angry to see all of the injustice in the world. She gently and wisely responded, "Why should I expend energy in anger that could be spent in love?"

3. Accept Who God Has Made You to Be

Many of anger's deep devastations are based in our inability to accept who we are. We wish for a different body with different hair, eyes, height, weight, nose, complexion, looks . . . We wish for different skills and abilities, whether artistic, mechanical, musical, mathematical, scientific . . . We wish we were smarter, prettier, stronger, cleverer, more agile, more . . . something. When we are unable to accept how God made us, with our strengths as well as our weaknesses, we are likely to develop deep resentments.

Not only do we get mad at God for having made us the way we are, but we develop jealous anger toward those who have or are what we want. We also get mad at ourselves for not being more like the person we wish we were. The lower our self-esteem, the higher our chances of getting angry—at life, situations, ourselves, and others, including God.

Have you ever stopped to think that maybe the source of some of your deepest problems is your own anger at yourself? In fact, people who are angry with themselves, often unknowingly, develop behaviors to punish themselves. Hendrie Weisinger puts it this way:

> When your anger has no place to go, and you do not know how to work it out, you experience the effects of self-anger. You make yourself look bad (obese), feel bad (depressed), act destructively

(excessive drinking), feel sick (migraine headaches), and do crazy things (commit suicide). People get angry at themselves for different reasons:

- I get angry at myself when I listen to somebody else's advice instead of following my own intuition.
- I get angry at myself when I eat too much.
- I get angry at myself for not doing as well as I know I can.
- I get angry at myself when I don't say how I really feel.
- I get angry at myself for making the same mistakes over and over.
- I get angry at myself for forgetting to do something.
- I get angry at myself for making a promise I don't want to keep.
- I get angry at myself for getting angry.[1]

It's okay to grieve the loss of something we don't have or can't be, but it isn't emotionally healthy to remain in our sadness. I (Becca) counseled a young man in his late twenties who had been diagnosed with severe depression. His depression was rooted in not being able to accept the fact that he would never be a great athlete. He was about five feet six and had always dreamed of (and even planned on) being a star basketball player. Rather than accept his limitations and revise his plans, he sunk deep into depression and remained there, wallowing in his anger at God for making him the way he was—short.

> **Have you ever stopped to think that maybe the source of some of your deepest problems is your own anger at yourself?**

The more able we are to admit and accept our limitations and imperfections, the better we will be at getting rid of deep, devastating anger.

What about you? Could some of your lingering, long-standing anger be rooted in your unwillingness to accept who you are and who you aren't? Do you need to grieve your loss before God, admit your disappointment, and confess your need to accept the "you" he made and designed for your good and his glory? He's waiting to lavish his love on you and tell you how wonderful he thinks you are.

> For you created my inmost being;
>   you knit me together in my mother's womb.
> I praise you because I am fearfully and wonderfully
>   made;
>   your works are wonderful,
>   I know that full well. My frame was not hidden from
>   you
>   when I was made in the secret place.
> When I was woven together in the depths of the earth,
>   your eyes saw my unformed body.
> All the days ordained for me
>   were written in your book
>   before one of them came to be.
>
> Ps. 139:13–16

4. Trust God: Let Him Be in Control

For many of us, the primary anger-producer in our lives is our inability to accept our circumstances. Accepting *who* we are is hard, but accepting *where* we are can be equally difficult. Anger is often germinated and nourished by our desire to have life be different or to have a different life. We want a different boss, mate, parent, friend, home, financial status, past, present, job, etc. We wish people would accept and love us better and treat us differently.

> He's waiting to lavish his love on you and tell you how wonderful he thinks you are.

Everyone has been unfairly treated, unjustly accused, and unkindly considered at some point in their life. We've had our toes stepped on, our feelings hurt, our pride pounced on, and our thoughts discounted. It hurts, and it's anger producing. But, as with all anger, we need to deal with it appropriately and then let it go. The more we dwell on the anger, the more it's likely to become our dwelling place.

God invites us to trust him—to let him help us rise above our painful circumstances and overcome our anger. When our lives seem out of control, he's the only one who can calm the raging storm within. Though we want full control over the course of our lives, that isn't possible. But we can trust him, let him be in charge, and rely on his sovereignty. After all, he *is* God.

> "To whom will you compare me?
>   Or who is my equal?" says the Holy One.
> Lift your eyes and look to the heavens:
>   Who created all these?
> He who brings out the starry host one by one,
>   and calls them each by name.
> Because of his great power and mighty strength,
>   not one of them is missing. . . . Do you not know?
>   Have you not heard?
> The LORD is the everlasting God,
>   the Creator of the ends of the earth.
> He will not grow tired or weary,
>   and his understanding no one can fathom.
>
> Isa. 40:25–26, 28

Numerous wonderful books have been written to encourage us to trust in God's sovereignty—to let God be God. He sees the big picture; we don't. He knows what is best for us; we don't. He knows what we can handle; we don't. He knows our thoughts and feelings better than we do ourselves. He understands what makes us tick and what ticks us off. He's ready and available to come to our aid and to guide us through life's rough roads. As the last verse above states, he will not grow tired or weary of helping us find our way through life.

5. Be a Grace Giver

This is a lesson God has been trying to teach me (Becca) for a long time. I would love for people to say that I was a gracious person, but unfortunately I have a long way to go. Being a grace giver means not getting uptight at others's imperfections, slowness, quirks, miscommunications, or lack of insight. It means that we give up a critical spirit fed by expectations, shoulds, and oughts and replace it with tolerance and understanding. That has the power to change lives—both yours and others'.

What does being a grace giver look like? Instead of grief, we give grace—a lot of freedom for people to be who they are and to make mistakes without someone coming down hard on them. Instead of criticizing, we hold our tongue. Instead of enforcing our rights, we back off. You and I long for others to be gracious toward us for our imperfections, yet too often we turn around and deprive others of graciousness. To be a grace giver, we must experience empathy and extend forgiveness. I have often heard grace defined as receiving something we don't deserve (like God's love and protection), whereas mercy is not receiving something we deserve (punishment and wrath). A grace giver offers both, being kind, forgiving, compassionate, and merciful. We cannot really understand grace, however, until we begin to experience the grace God has lavished upon us. And once we do, our lives begin to be transformed, and so do the lives of people around us as they experience God's grace through us.

Dr. Paul Tournier, an insightful Swiss psychiatrist, wrote numerous books well worth reading. One of them that we recommend particularly highly is *Guilt and Grace*, in which he suggests that as Christians more fully realize their imperfect nature and become disillusioned and discouraged by their perpetual sin, they then begin to fathom God's grace. "It is then that we understand more profoundly how vast the grace is which receives us just as we are, with all our despair, all our weaknesses, and all our relapses."[2]

God has demonstrated grace to us throughout history. Jesus showed us what grace meant when he welcomed sinners at his table, when he touched a banished leper, when he forgave an adulteress, when he allowed children to come, when he told of the forgiven, restored prodigal son, when he spoke of the persistent woman, when he healed the sick, when he fed the multitudes, and much more. He is a God who spared sin-ridden Nineveh, who loved an adulterous and idolatrous people, and who used murderers and liars for his glory. His grace accepts the weak and the strong, the sinner and the upright, and the prodigal as well as the faithful. This is the grace for which we should all aspire.

6. Be a Person of Prayer

The more we pray, the more we are filled with love and compassion and the less room we have for destructive anger. When we pray, we are often transformed to greater heights. We see our problems from a different vantage point, and they suddenly seem a lot smaller and less significant. Prayer lifts us into God's presence where we begin to see things from his perspective.

> Prayer lifts us into God's presence where we begin to see things from his perspective.

Rather than focusing on our hurts, praying for the needs of those around us can have a powerful effect. We develop greater empathy for the struggles and failures of others. Anger loses its stinging power—one reason that God's Word calls us to pray for those who mistreat us (Luke 6:28). We even begin to forget our own offenses and focus more on the needs of others.

In prayer, we sense God's heart and begin to see through his eyes. He asks us to change our view from self-righteousness to righteousness: "Whatever is true, whatever is noble, whatever is right, whatever is pure, whatever is lovely, whatever is admirable—if anything is excellent or praiseworthy—think about such things" (Phil. 4:8). If our thoughts are full of what is true, noble, right, pure, lovely, admirable, and worthy of praise, then angry thoughts get crowded out.

Recap

These anger-reduction and anger-prevention tasks have focused on ways to change your lifestyle and attitudes so that you're less likely to get angry. The keys to lessening anger's grip on your life are to minimize stress and maximize God. This means you'll need to eliminate hurry, downsize your expectations, admit mistakes, laugh more, take care of yourself, and know more of what triggers your anger. It also means that you'll need to get right with God, experience his lavish love, accept who he made you to be, trust in him and his sovereignty, and be a gracious person who prays. Sound easy? It isn't. But if you commit to this challenge to change, it can be done. With God, all things are possible.

The Bottom Line

The more we allow God's love to infiltrate every fiber of our being, the less room there is for anger to reside. Fewer things will anger us as we begin to see ourselves as God does, accept who we are, learn to trust him, and become more gracious and prayerful people.

Here's a summary of the Anger Reduction Lifestyle tasks:

Anger Reduction Lifestyle (Anger Prevention), Parts 1 and 2

Minimize Stress
1. Eliminate hurry.
2. Downsize expectations.
3. Learn to say no.
4. Admit mistakes and imperfections.
5. Laugh more—don't take life or yourself too seriously.
6. Take care of yourselves.
7. Know what triggers your anger.

Maximize God
1. Get right with God: believe in him, confess your sins, forgive others.
2. Experience God's unconditional love and acceptance.
3. Accept who God made you to be.
4. Trust God and his sovereignty—let him be in control.
5. Be a grace giver.
6. Be a person of prayer.

Questions to Consider

1. Have you experienced a time when your angry attitude was transformed due to a new or changed perspective? If so, what did you learn from that process? If not, what have you learned in this chapter that could help?

2. What things do you wish were different in your life? What degree of anger do you sense as a result of those things?

3. In what ways might God's love change your perspective on yourself if it really sank into your heart? In what ways might his sovereignty do the same if your mind could truly grasp it?

4. How do you think God wants you to respond to him right now?

Action Steps to Take

- Write down which anger-reducing tasks from each list you most need to work on and which ways you can improve in these areas.
- Ask a trusted friend or family member to role-play a situation with you in which that person makes biting, sarcastic, or insulting comments to you—the more outrageous and unrealistic, the better. Practice speaking words of grace and understanding to that person. Though the exercise may seem farfetched, the simple act of refusing anger and voicing grace will begin to establish lasting habits in you.
- Pray this "God-maximizing" prayer every morning for the next week:

Lord, you've suffered more offenses than anyone in the history of the world, and some of those offenses have come from me. You have more right than anyone to be angry and to withhold grace, yet you lavish your love on even the worst of sinners. Thank you. I declare my complete trust in your promise to work all things together for good and to execute justice in the right way at the right time. Help me to continually cast that responsibility off on you and, in the place of my anger, to be an extravagant grace giver. Let me see the power of grace to change my life and the lives of others. Amen.

PART 7

HOW TO BE
GOOD AND MAD

19

Express Anger

Anger should be a stepping stone, not a stumbling block.

In an earlier chapter I (Chip) mentioned the time when I saw a woman in a laundromat throw her young child against a dryer. I witnessed it shortly after I got out of seminary. Everything in me wanted to give that woman a taste of her own medicine. I watched as that mother banged her little daughter into a dryer and screamed in her precious face. In my mind, I can still see that little arm being jerked. I told the woman, "In my presence, ma'am, don't you ever treat that child like that again."

I was mad. I was so mad I couldn't sleep. I thought, *That's most likely going to happen to that child again—probably a lot. It's a pattern. And what kind of parent is she going to become if she's treated like that all her life? Probably a lot like her mom.* I remember lying awake and being furious. Adrenalin pumped through my system. *How many hundreds of kids are experiencing this day after day, night after night?* I thought. *God, this can't go on. I'm going to do something. I don't know what, but I'm going to do something.*

I found out that there was a child welfare board in our county. It was one of those groups with committee after committee where someone is supposed to do something, but hardly anything ever really happens. When I shared my concerns, they said, "Since you're concerned, why don't you serve on the board?"

"Yes, that would be great," I said.

"Okay, you're chairman."

I didn't hesitate long before saying, "Okay." I started recruiting my friends, asking them if they wanted to "make a difference." We got a team of people together, and before long we built a shelter for abused kids. Churches in the area gave food and provided temporary housing. We trained foster parents and taught anger management seminars. The whole county began to network and work together. Whenever a problem arose and a child was hurt, I would share from the pulpit, "I need size 2 clothes for a little boy and size 4 for a little girl. We also have three little kids who need somewhere to go for a few weeks." Sure enough, someone in the church would have the clothes, and a family would say, "We'll take the kids." We teamed up with other churches and made a difference. Why? Because I got mad—not just a little mad—fuming mad!

We've spent most of the book so far focusing on how to understand, prevent, contain, and control anger. But as we shared before, not all anger is bad; it also has a constructive, positive side. In fact, according to the Bible, we are commanded to be angry. Most Scripture verses on anger admonish us to beware of the potential hazards of anger, but in Ephesians 4:26–27, we're told not only that it's allowed but that we're *supposed* to get angry. "Be angry but do not sin; do not let the sun go down on your anger, and do not make room for the devil" (NRSV). Anger is one of the most positive, effective weapons in the arsenal of God to bring about radical, righteous change—in the believer, in the church, and in society. There are times when the most appropriate thing to do is get mad. It's natural and it's needed.

This command to "be angry" comes with three conditions: (1) do not sin; (2) do not let the sun go down on your anger; and (3) do not make room for the devil. That is, resolve it. The verse doesn't say, "Do not get angry," but rather, "be angry." We are immediately warned, however, that it's easy to let our anger lead to sin. Therefore, "be angry *but* do not sin." Then we're commanded to resolve our anger, to not let it smolder and stew. Why? Be-cause that gives room to the devil (v. 27). God knows that if our anger is improperly motivated, and if it lingers, it gives the "enemy" the opportunity to reside in our hearts. Anger turns into bitterness and resentment. This is one of the ways that "your enemy the devil prowls around like a roaring lion looking for someone to devour" (1 Peter 5:8).

> Anger is one of the most positive, effective weapons in the arsenal of God to bring about radical, righteous change.

Here's a summary of the verse:

Ephesians 4:26–27

Verse		The Command and the Conditions
"Be angry"		Express anger
"But do not sin"	*but*	Express anger appropriately
"Do not let the sun go down on your anger."	*and*	Resolve anger

So it's true that God commands us to express our anger, but he also provides additional conditions. In part 4 we looked at James 1 and God's *plan* in dealing with anger. Now we look at God's *command* regarding anger from Ephesians 4.

Why Are We Given This Command?

Before we take a deeper look at the command and conditions, let's see when and why it was written. We're told in those two verses to be angry, to be careful not to sin, and to resolve our anger. What's the context in which Paul, inspired by the Holy Spirit, wrote to the Ephesian church? What preceded and motivated these instructions?

The first three chapters of Ephesians are about doctrine. They tell us who we are in Christ. The last three chapters tell us how to live in Christ. Chapter 4 begins with a transitional statement: "I urge you to live (lead) a life worthy." Another translation reads, "walk worthy" (KJV). We are instructed to live in a way that is worthy and good and right. Then we find the goal of this lifestyle: "so that the body of Christ may be built up until we all reach unity in the faith and in the knowledge of the Son of God and become mature, attaining to the whole measure of the fullness of Christ" (4:12–13). We are to build up one another, to be unified, to know the Son of God, to become spiritually mature—that is, to become more like Jesus.

To become more like Jesus, we'll need to stop living the way we used to. That requires a radical transformation. How? We renew our minds. We put off (discard) the old self (our former lifestyle) with its corruption and sinful desires, and put on the new self by the renewal of our mind (4:22–24).

The very next word after this instruction is "Therefore" (4:25). This lets us know we're about to be given some practical steps on how to live out the new lifestyle day by day. From this point forward, we're taught the "how-to" of a Christlike life. In a sense, Paul writes, "Stop doing this. Start doing this. Do this. Don't do that. Replace this negative. Institute this positive. Have your mind renewed."

The verses that follow talk about honesty, anger, giving, and our words and attitudes. We are told to speak truthfully and not to lie (4:25). Then come our instructions on anger (4:26–27). After that, "do not steal," but instead work at something useful to contribute to those in need (4:28). Verse 29 instructs us to encourage others and not to let any unwholesome words come out of our mouths. We are reminded not to "grieve the Holy Spirit" in verse 30. And we are given clear guidelines for our attitudes: "Get rid of all bitterness, rage and anger, brawling and slander, along with every form of malice" (4:31). Those are the "don'ts." Then come the "dos." "Be kind and compassionate to one another, forgiving each other, just as in Christ God forgave you" (4:32).

Here's a chart summarizing the context and these dos and don'ts.

An Overview of Ephesians

Chapters 1–3	Who we are in Christ
Chapters 4–6	How to live in Christ

The Context of Ephesians 4:26–27

Chapter/ Verse	Content	
Chapter 4		
4:1	Live (walk) in a godly (worthy) manner.	
4:12–13	Seek maturity (live a godly life).	
4:17	Stop living an ungodly life.	
4:22–24	How to live a godly life:	
	Renew your mind.	
	Put off the old self with its old ways.	
4:25	*Therefore:*	
	(now the practical, specific "how tos" of living a godly life)	
4:25–31	*Do*	*Don't*
4:25	Speak the truth.	Don't lie.

Chapter/ Verse	Content	
4:26–27	Be angry.	Don't sin in your anger.
	Don't let your anger go unresolved.	
4:28	Share, contribute, be useful.	Don't steal.
4:29	Edify, encourage.	Don't let unwholesome (unedifying) words come from your mouth.
4:30–31	Be kind, tenderhearted, forgiving.	Don't have malice, bitterness, slander, rage, or brawling.

Though our book focuses on anger and, therefore, on the challenges and commands of 4:26–27, dealing with anger is not the point of this passage. Please don't miss this point. Verses 26–27 are not just about having more control over our anger, although that is one result. Neither are they simply about how to have better emotional health and get along with others. That will happen if we deal with anger biblically. More importantly, however, this passage was written to help us become more righteous—more like Christ individually and corporately—so that we transform not only our minds but also our culture. The context of these verses is to be angry and not sin in order for our lives to achieve and promote individual and corporate righteousness.

Be Angry!

Many children are safer and happier because I got mad in the laundromat that day many years ago. On many occasions, anger is good and produces good results. History is full of far-reaching examples, such as William Wilberforce, whose anger over the injustice of slavery prompted him to begin unraveling England's laws that allowed it, and Martin Luther, whose anger over gross distortions of the gospel eventually catalyzed an entire reformation. Unfortunately, there are also many instances in which anger has been stifled and stuffed, and no positive changes have resulted.

Our challenge is to express our anger the right way. God commands us to. Too many of us don't get angry when we should. If and when we do feel it, we don't express it. Ephesians 4:26 tells us not only that anger is okay but that it should be expressed.

> On many occasions, anger is good and produces good results.

How did we become so afraid to feel or express anger? Perhaps we fear reproach or disapproval from others if we show anger. Or perhaps we fear becoming an uncontrollable monster. Whatever the source of our fear, we need to overcome it so we can express anger when we should. If we can't, we inadvertently contribute to the continuance of injustice and unrighteousness.

Thought-provoking theologian John Stott affirms this: "This verse recognizes that there is such a thing as Christian anger, and too few Christians either feel or express it. Indeed, when we fail to do so, we deny God, damage ourselves, and encourage the spread of evil."[1]

The Bottom Line

There are many times, contrary to popular belief, when being angry and expressing it are godly responses. In many instances, we need to be angry more, not less. Anger is one of the most positive, effective weapons in the arsenal of God to bring about radical, righteous change, not only in the believer and in the church, but also in society. We are challenged and commanded to be angry.

Questions to Consider

1. Can you think of a time when you felt bad about getting angry, only to realize that your anger was good and appropriate? How have you overcome any false guilt associated with such anger?
2. What fears and hindrances keep you from expressing anger at the right times for the right reasons?
3. Is there an issue or injustice or situation that really makes you angry? Could God be speaking to you about turning that anger into action?

Action Steps to Take

- If you grew up thinking that it was wrong to express anger, one of the best ways you can retrain yourself to accept anger as a valid and necessary reaction is to identify how others have used it constructively. Look for one opportunity this week to affirm someone whose anger leads them to appropriate action. Also consider reading biographies of Martin Luther, William Wilberforce, and other anger "activists" to help establish this truth in your mind.
- Identify what injustice in our world (and specifically in your sphere of influence) most angers you. Then determine one step you could take this week to make a positive difference in that situation.
- Identify at least one person you would like to join you in setting this injustice right. Arrange to meet this person for a cup of coffee and discuss a plan of action.

20

Express Anger
Appropriately

Unholy tempers are always unhappy tempers.
—John Wesley

In 1980 a loving mother got angry. Someone who had too much to drink—he had been on a three-day binge—veered off of a neighborhood road and struck a thirteen-year-old girl. The life of this mother's young teenager was instantly snuffed out. The mother, Candice Lightner, was devastated, ripped open by grief. But after she grieved, she got mad—*really* mad. She did research and found that there were more deaths every single year in alcohol-related accidents in America than all the young men killed in Vietnam. She was enraged. She decided immediately to start MADD—Mothers Against Drunk Driving. It may have started small, but there are now chapters all over the United States. The organization has lobbied hard, and laws have been changed. Largely due to the efforts of MADD, thousands of lives have been saved—all because a heartbroken, angry woman let her anger be known.[1]

Candice Lightner didn't seek revenge against the drunk driver who killed her daughter. She didn't lash out and destroy property or people. Nor did she remain in her grief, stuffing the anger deep down inside. She didn't self-destruct. Instead, she expressed her anger. She got it out appropriately in ways that were constructive rather than destructive. That's what we're commanded to do.

> **Our anger must be strong, caring, understanding, and under control.**

Those who find it hard to express anger at all certainly face a challenge in expressing it appropriately. As we've noted, the commandment to be angry is accompanied by two conditions. The first requires a righteous response. We need to get mad yet not sin. That means being assertive rather than aggressive, confronting rather than combative, responsive rather than reactive. Our anger must be strong, caring, understanding, and under control.

Surprisingly, a number of New Testament stories point us toward an encouraging example of this dynamic: Jesus.[2] Far from the passive, melancholy, always-gentle portrayal we see in popular culture and Hollywood films, Jesus expressed the full range of human emotions freely but without sin. And those emotions included some pretty strong expressions of anger on more than one occasion.

Jesus's Example of Expressing Anger Appropriately

We can see several situations in the New Testament in which Jesus was angry. In Mark 3 he was *visibly angry*. Jesus entered a synagogue and saw a disabled man. The text says, "They watched him closely to see if he would heal him." It continues, "He looked around at them in anger and . . . said to the man, 'Stretch out your hand'... and his hand was completely restored" (vv. 2–5). When the religious leaders saw what Jesus did on the Sabbath, they rebuked and despised him for not following the strict religious laws of the time. These religious men had gotten so caught up in all of their rules that they missed the truth. Jesus disobeyed their interpretation of the law because he knew it was not what God had intended. The true law allowed one to do good, to heal, to feed, to love—regardless of the day. He was fuming at the narrow-minded, legalistic, self-seeking, hypocritical superficiality of the religious leaders.

Jesus was also *verbally angry*. In Matthew 23 we read some of the harshest words in Scripture. Jesus addressed this same group of religious leaders, directly calling them "hypocrites," "a brood of vipers," "blind guides," and "snakes."

> Woe to you, teachers of the law and Pharisees, you hypocrites! You give a tenth of your spices—mint, dill and cumin. But you have neglected the more important matters of the law—justice, mercy and faithfulness. You should have practiced the latter, without neglecting the former. You blind guides! You strain out a gnat but swallow a camel. Woe to you, teachers of the law and Pharisees, you hypocrites! You clean the outside of the cup and dish, but inside they are full of greed and self-indulgence.... Woe to you, teachers of the law and Pharisees, you hypocrites! You are like whitewashed tombs, which look beautiful on the outside but on the inside are full of dead men's bones and everything unclean. In the same way, on the outside you appear to people as righteous but on the inside you are full of hypocrisy and wickedness.... You snakes! You brood of vipers! How will you escape being condemned to hell? (Matt. 23:23–25, 27–28, 33)

Those are strong, anger-filled words—some of the strongest ever written, and they came out of the mouth of Jesus, the Son of God and the "Prince of Peace." He was speaking to the

Pharisees and Sadducees, a group of religious leaders. When Jesus saw their inconsistency, hypocrisy, lack of integrity, and pretension, he was indignant. He got angry, but his anger was under control.

In Mark 11, we read that Jesus was *physically angry*.

On reaching Jerusalem, Jesus entered the temple area and began driving out those who were buying and selling there. He overturned the tables of the money changers and the benches of those selling doves, and would not allow anyone to carry merchandise through the temple courts. And as he taught them, he said, "Is it not written: 'My house will be called a house of prayer for all nations'? But you have made it 'a den of robbers.'" (Mark 11:15–7)

As Jesus entered the holy temple of God, he saw people who were charging exorbitant prices for religious items—making money illegitimately in the name of God. They were greedily exploiting those who had come to worship. Jesus saw this defilement of the temple and got mad—*really* mad. He was furious that people were not treating God's holy place with honor and respect. He went in with a whip in his hand and displayed his anger physically yet appropriately. He turned over the tables, he pushed things away, and he drove out the animals. It wasn't rage. He didn't become the Incredible Hulk, grabbing someone and throwing him across the room. He was not going berserk. He was physically angry but still under control.

Jesus's Response When Attacked Unfairly

From these passages, we read how Jesus became quite angry over the injustices and misguided perspectives of the day. But how did he respond when personally attacked? When there was wrong behavior, He was forceful, direct, and under control. When he was personally attacked, however, He didn't respond with threats or whips. What did he do? He remained quiet. He gave it to God the Father. He found no need to justify himself. He didn't get defensive or insecure, start gossiping, become passive aggressive, or erupt in explosive outbursts. He saw it from a heavenly perspective and responded with quiet calm and peaceful assurance that God is sovereign and in control.

> Jesus became quite angry over the injustices and misguided perspectives of the day.

Some have remarked that the Bible often tells us to defend the rights of others (see Isaiah 58 for a strong statement of this) while never telling us to defend our own. That's the pattern we see in Jesus, who was zealous about the welfare of other people and seemingly unconcerned for his own welfare. If he is our example—and he is—then this is how we should express our sense of justice as well.

A Fourth Anger Profile: Expressing Anger Appropriately

It's an overwhelming challenge to respond to anger as Jesus did. As humans, we tend to spew, stuff, or leak our anger, which we've examined in earlier chapters. If these ways of responding to anger are unhealthy, then how *should* we respond to anger? How can we respond appropriately—in ways that are more similar than dissimilar to Jesus's responses?

> Jesus became quite angry over the injustices and misguided perspectives of the day.

Let's review the three common anger profiles, adding a fourth one that we label simply as "Appropriate Expression."

231

Responses to Anger

Area	Stuff	Spew	Leak	Appropriate Expression
Message to onself when angry	"I must not show anger, or be angry, because anger is bad."	"It's your fault." "Anger is necessary."	"It's too dangerous to express anger directly." "Showing anger is bad."	"It is okay to be angry. It's what I do with it that matters." (Eph. 4:26–27) "Anger can be good."
Action	Stuff, avoid, pretend Repress Suppress	Explode, control Uncontrolled Controlling	Passive-aggressive Indirect power Direct, subtle slander	Be assertive. Make non-threatening "I" statements about needs and desires.
Reaction	Deny feeling angry Bury, hide anger Pretend you're not angry	Yell, slam doors, shout, hit, kick, push, put down, become hostile	Procrastinate, be late, gossip, don't follow through, "yes" and "no" are unreliable	Express it directly or release it indirectly, getting the anger out in nondestructive ways
Results	Grow out of touch with emotions, live in denial, expend excessive energy avoiding anger	Damaged relationships, emotional distancing	Unhealthy communication patterns, damaged relationships	Restored, healthy relationships, open, honest communication, justice and righteousness upheld, grace and mercy given

When we express our anger appropriately, we learn to communicate our needs and concerns clearly. We use "I" statements rather than hurl accusations; redirect excess anger in healthy ways; extend grace, mercy, love, and forgiveness; and get angry at what really matters.

Right Motives and Methods

Aristotle is credited with saying, "Anybody can become angry—that is easy; but to be angry with the right person, to the right degree, at the right time, for the right purpose, and in the right way—that is not within everybody's power and is not easy." Our anger needs to be motivated for the right reasons, responded to appropriately, and resolved quickly.

Appropriate anger requires having the right motives and the right methods.

Appropriate anger requires having the right motives and the right methods. It's possible to be mad for the right reason but to express that anger sinfully. It's also possible to be mad for the wrong reason but to deal with it appropriately. Those who are opposed to abortion, for example, strongly believe that their reason for anger is justified. But when the few radicals begin blowing up abortion clinics, they have stepped over the line. Though they feel they have the right motivation, they have used the wrong method. The way to respond to a "just" cause is by either expressing (communicating and verbalizing) our concerns or seeking ways to re-direct and release our feelings. Such a response might also include a call to action and prayer. When we are motivated for the wrong reasons, an appropriate response would be to let it go.

The following chart helps illustrate this "Motivation–Methods" difference.

Motivation (Reason)	Method (Response)	
	Appropriate Response	*Inappropriate Response*
Right reasons	Express or release Prayer and action	Spew, stuff, or leak Harmful behavior
Wrong reasons	Let it go	Reacting in an unhealthy way

Appropriate anger is generated from right reasons. It is not anger born from selfishness, pride, or insecurities. We express it appropriately when we communicate or redirect it in non-threatening, nondestructive ways.

What Healthy, Appropriate Anger Looks Like

Much psychological research verifies the wisdom of God's perspective and plan. We experience healthy, constructive anger when we:

1. are quick to hear (hearing others, our primary feelings, and God)
2. are slow to speak
3. are slow to anger
4. express it (rather than stifle or ignore it)
5. express it appropriately (express or redirect it, having the right motives and methods)
6. resolve it

The Bottom Line

Expressing anger may not be too difficult a command to follow, but to express it *appropriately* is a much harder task. Jesus is our example. We know that it can be destructive to stuff, spew, or leak our anger. Expressing anger appropriately requires that we follow Jesus's example and God's anger recommendations and requirements found in James 1:19–20 and Ephesians 4:26–27.

Questions to Consider

1. Are you comfortable with the fact that Jesus expressed anger harshly at times? Why or why not?

2. Think of a situation in which you expressed anger clearly but inappropriately. After reading this chapter, how would you handle that situation differently?

3. If you had to rate yourself on the six aspects of healthy anger, what would your strongest areas be? Your weakest?

Action Steps to Take

- Read and meditate on John 2:13–17, another version of the story we read in Mark 11.

- In light of the biblical passages about Jesus cited in this chapter, develop a list of criteria that define the differences between healthy, righteous anger and destructive, unrighteous anger.

- Choose one of the items listed as healthy anger, and devise a plan for how you will work to improve that area in your life this week.

- Whom do you know who could relate to what you've been learning about healthy anger? Call or meet that person this week and share your journey.

21

Resolve Anger

> All anger is not sinful, but it becomes sinful and contradicts Scripture when it . . . continues long.
>
> —William Paley

I thought we were friends. He arranged a time for a phone call to discuss a situation. He had some misinformation and thought I was involved in it in some way or another. I later learned that he recorded the conversation in order to play it to a group of people. By the grace of God, I hadn't said anything that was untrue or incriminating. When I heard what he did, I was livid. The level of betrayal and deceit wounded me deeply. I wasn't mad; I was livid. I fantasized about what I would do if I acted on my seething anger. I couldn't sleep. I had knots in my stomach. My chest pounded when I ate. I drank a lot of coffee. I was a mess.

I said to myself, "I've got to deal with this. I'm a Christian and a pastor. It's going to be hard to preach this weekend with this attitude." So I decided to write a letter letting him know what I'd found out, how he was wrong, and that I'd forgiven him (though he didn't deserve it). At least that was the tone of it.

At lunch a close friend saw that I was struggling. I told him about the letter and how sending it would be like putting a nail in the coffin; it would end the matter. He asked to see the letter. Being a good friend, I expected him to affirm me, call the person a jerk, and tell me to let him have it. Instead, he responded, "I think you've been wronged, and it's been blatant. But I think what's really been wounded is your pride, and I think your response is a proud one. I think the reputation you're really concerned about is not God's as much as it is yours. And I think what you're really stressed about is what people will think."

My friend affirmed that I'd been wronged, and he affirmed our friendship, but he also challenged and confronted me. He told me to keep the letter in my briefcase until I could rewrite it without any hidden, accusative, inferring messages, and until I could truly forgive him and be able to pray for God's blessing in his life despite the pain I was experiencing. He gently reminded me that when Jesus had been unfairly attacked, he didn't retaliate. He quoted 1 Peter: "For it is commendable if a man bears up under the pain of unjust suffering because he is conscious of God. . . . If you suffer for doing good and you endure it, this is commendable before God. To this you were called, because Christ suffered for you, leaving you an example, that you should follow in his steps. When they hurled their insults at him, he did not retaliate; when he suffered, he made no threats. Instead, he entrusted himself to him who judges justly" (1 Peter 2:19–21, 23).

My wise friend told me I needed to confess my response as sinful and repent and ask God to forgive me. Ouch! It hurt to clean out the debris, but it was essential. And eventually it was effective in bringing about emotional healing.

God commands us to resolve our anger. He knows that if we don't, it festers; and like a terminal disease, it will destroy us. If anger isn't dealt with, it eats us up inside.

Here's an overview of the verse once more:

Ephesians 4:26–27

Verse		The Command and the Conditions
"Be angry"		Express anger
"But do not sin"	*but*	Express anger appropriately
"Do not let the sun go down on your anger."	*and*	Resolve anger

Unresolved anger can literally destroy us *physically* as we internalize the feelings. We develop intestinal problems, muscle strain, ulcers, colitis, and headaches, among other maladies. We become more easily fatigued and stressed. When our anger level is high, our physical and emotional tolerance level is low.

Unresolved anger can also destroy us *emotionally* as we feed the festering fiend inside. Anger grows into bitter resentment, the roots of which dig deep down into the soil of our soul. We become lonely and alienated. Our attempts at emotional payback usually boomerang, coming back to hurt us in the long run. Withdrawing from and ignoring the person who hurt us often leaves us feeling like the outsider when we've allowed anger rather than reconciliation to guide our behavior.

> **Unresolved anger can literally destroy us *physically* as we internalize the feelings.**

Our hurts may be superficial, or they may be deep. They may be a fleeting event or an inescapable ongoing situation. They may be coldly impersonal or painfully personal. They may involve a stranger or a loved one. Whatever the depth, the cause, or the consequences, we need to get rid of the anger by resolving it as quickly as possible.

How do we do that? How can we heal the hurt? How do we confront someone or deal with something so volatile and potentially explosive? Let's examine what keeps us from resolving anger, learn practical "rules" to follow, and understand God's perspective on the importance of finding resolution.

Identify What Keeps Us from Resolving Our Anger

Before we jump into the importance of resolving our anger and what God recommends, it would be wise to take a quick look at what keeps us from dealing with our anger. Here are four main reasons:

1. We want to keep our anger as a form of payback or revenge. To let go of our anger is to forgive the person—to let them off the hook—and we're not ready or willing to do that. (Refer also to the earlier list of the misuses of anger, or why we keep anger around, from chapter 2.)
2. We are extremely apprehensive and fearful of confrontation. Our motto is "Don't make waves" or "Peace at all costs," and that peace is usually paid for by our nonconfrontive, internal combustion.
3. We feel apathetic, sure that any attempt at resolution would end in defeat. We believe that dealing with the issue would only "make matters worse," and we'd end up feeling like a loser.
4. For a variety of reasons, we put our heads in the sand and pretend the problem doesn't really exist. We decide that the best course of action is no action. Instead of dealing with it, we run from it. Though there are times when it's best to put our attempts at resolution on hold, some people do so indefinitely because of their fears and denial of a problem.

Do any of these describe you? If so, consider that resolution is not an option. God commands it. Why? Because he knows it will eventually destroy us and our relationships with him and others. We must overcome these roadblocks if we are to obey.

Conflict Resolution

Much has been written on the subject of conflict resolution, and a multitude of seminars have been offered to help people with it. Different people emphasize different aspects and different approaches, but the goal is always the same—to resolve the conflict.

Several years ago I (Becca) had a phone fight with my sister. I don't even remember what the argument was about, but I vividly remember the intensity of emotions. When we hung up, I replayed in my head what *she* had done and what *she* had said over and over again. I began to identify all of the areas in which *she* had "hit below the belt," writing them down as I went. I decided to write her a letter politely informing her how she had fought unfairly. Fortunately, before I sent it I asked a close friend to read it. I expected her to tell me how mature and objective the letter was. Instead, she told me that I myself had violated several of the unfair practices of which I was accusing my attacker. Ouch!

These "rules," as I began to call them, are practical steps toward conflict resolution. They are especially helpful in the midst of an argument to keep it from becoming an all-out war in which anger provides the ammunition. But they can also be useful when we return to a conflict to resolve it. They are preventative, practical, and imperative.

Below is an abbreviated version of a list called "The Rules of Fair Fighting" I have developed and refined. Breaking these rules leads to intensified anger; following them helps subdue and resolve it.

Fighting Fair

To disagree is one thing; to be disagreeable is another.

Whatever you call it—an argument, fight, difference of opinion, quarrel, conflict, disagreement, debate, or dispute—we should know the rules of fair fighting. Of course, knowing these guidelines isn't enough. We must follow them. So what are they?

When you find yourself in an argument:

1. Deal with the present issue only.
2. Refrain from using words like "always" and "never."
3. Examine yourself—your motives, mood, and feelings.
4. Control your temper.
5. Try to understand the other person's position and feelings.
6. Use "I" words rather than "you" statements.
7. Stick to the issues and don't attack the other person's character.
8. Listen.
9. Remain open-minded.
10. Don't make statements that negate any possible response—that trap, corner, box, or hem the person in.
11. Assume innocence until proven guilty rather than vice versa.
12. When fighting, be aware of the surroundings and those nearby, and do so as privately as possible.
13. Stick to the content of the argument, not the process or the person.
14. After the argument, don't recount it to others in an effort to gain allies.
15. Be willing to compromise.
16. Be willing to admit weaknesses and mistakes and to say, "I'm sorry."

The apostle Paul advised Titus to "avoid foolish controversies . . . and arguments and quarrels . . . because these are unprofitable and useless" (Titus 3:9). This wise advice also applies to us today.

Here's the key: Your temper is one of your most valuable possessions. Don't lose it.

Resolve It Quickly

"Anyone who is angry with his brother will be subject to judgment. . . . Therefore, if you are offering your gift at the altar and there remember that your brother has something against you, leave your gift there in front of the altar. First go and be reconciled to your brother; then come and offer your gift. Settle matters quickly" (Matt. 5:22–25).

According to this verse, we are "subject to judgment" when we get angry. The criteria by which our anger is judged is whether it's appropriate or inappropriate, self-righteous or righteously motivated. This verse ends with a mandate: "Settle matters quickly," or work them out expediently. The command in Ephesians also indicates that we are to get rid of our anger quickly—before the sun goes down. Why? Because God knows that we have a tendency to let anger linger. Many of us prefer to harbor anger, avoid confrontation, give in, or pretend. When we run from it, however, we also avoid the possibility of resolution.

> When we run from it, however, we also avoid the possibility of resolution.

This applies regardless of the depth of the wound. "Oh, but what my parents did to me! I'm so mad! What my ex-mate did to me! My kids—what they put me through! My boss, he ripped me off for so much money!" *It's okay to be angry—but it's not okay to befriend it. Anger is meant to be a passing acquaintance, not a longtime, live-in companion.*

Why Should You Resolve Anger?

I had harbored anger way too long. The target of my anger was a person who had made some decisions with which I didn't agree, had neglected to communicate some key information to me, and had left me out of some other decisions in which

I thought I should have been included. In my typical leaking fashion, I sought ways to gently blast this person. What were the emotions underlying my anger? Pride, rejection, self-absorption, and jealousy—to name a few! It was eating me up inside. The thought of the person caused my stomach to do cartwheels. I didn't want to pray about it, because I knew I'd have to forgive the person, and I really didn't want to. When I finally allowed God to penetrate my stubborn heart, he gently but firmly reminded me of *my* sinfulness and the need to resolve my growing, festering anger. I broke down and wept.

I then spent a lot of time in prayer asking God to clarify what my issues were, where I needed to extend forgiveness, and where I needed to ask for forgiveness. When I finally went to see the person, I was able to clearly communicate my concerns, taking responsibility for my own feelings and reactions. At times the person was apologetic, at times defensive. Misunderstandings, miscommunications, and intentions were clarified or explained. How did I feel walking out of that office? Great! It felt like an enormous weight had been lifted off my shoulders. The skip was back in my step, the gleam back in my eye. The stinging anger had disappeared. I inwardly chastised my foolish self for my disobedience to God's Word and for taking so very long to get rid of the anger. Resolving the anger felt so good.

We've already mentioned that unresolved anger can adversely affect us both emotionally and physically. If not dealt with, it will have negative consequences on our body, our relationships, our work performance, and our emotional well-being. We also know that it hinders our coming before God. But there's another important reason in addition to these: if we don't resolve our anger, it gives Satan "a foothold." That's how Ephesians 4:26–27 reads: "Do not let the sun go down while you are still angry, and do not give the devil a foothold." If we don't resolve things quickly, we're opening the door just wide enough for the enemy

Anger gives the devil time.

to slip his foot in. Just a crack makes it easier for him to get in. Opening the door to the destructive power of anger—even just a little—invites a terrible, potentially terminal monster to reside within our hearts.

This is one of the most vulnerable areas in which the enemy gets into our lives. Anger festers into bitterness and resentment. There's a saying that "anger gives the devil time." If we don't resolve it, we're in danger of hardening into an angry person.

Have you ever read *The Screwtape Letters* by C. S. Lewis? It's a delightfully entertaining book chronicling letters sent from a senior demon to a younger apprentice. The letters give instructions on how to entice humans away from godly pursuits. The subordinate feels like a failure when the human under his supervision becomes a Christian. His supervisor quickly informs him that this could be turned into an advantage because the person is now more likely to be sensitive to guilt and anger. If the person experiences anger, he is more likely to focus on that than on godliness. And it's true: We much too easily get caught up in our anger and lose sight of what's really important. "Satan knows how to exploit anger. . . . Once he has us nursing and justifying our selfish anger, he knows we are not far from hatred, revenge, a refusal to forgive, and violence."[1]

God commands us to resolve our anger before bedtime because he knows the enemy wants us to focus on little things that personally affect us. Satan knows that if the church of Jesus Christ ever gets angry and ticked off about sin, wickedness, and injustice, he's got problems.[2]

We seek to resolve anger not just to keep Satan out but also, according to the passage in Matthew 5, because it leads to the possibility of reconciliation and restored relationships. We are to "go and be reconciled" to our brother.

We are also told that not resolving an offense interferes with our relationship with God. We must go and make things right with others before we can come before God. Spiritually, unresolved anger gets in our way. In order to have unobstructed worship, we need to make wrong things right. Resolving anger not only shuts Satan out, but it opens wide the door to unhindered worship of God. The verse in Matthew informs us that once we have taken care of the problem, we can again return to God's holy temple.

Unresolved anger breaks relationships, allows Satan a foothold, and interrupts our fellowship with God.

Here's a simple chart summarizing this command and the positive results we achieve when we resolve our anger:

Commands:	Results:
Resolve anger.	Satan won't get a foothold.
Resolve anger quickly.	We reconcile with our "brother."
	We can return to unhindered worship.

Matt. 5:22–25; Eph. 4:26–27

How Do You Know If It's Unresolved?

How can you know if you have unresolved anger? If hearing a name or recalling an event causes you to feel flushed, your blood pressure to rise, knots to tighten in your stomach, and your heart to race, that's a pretty good indication you're nursing an old wound. When left unresolved, anger moves from righteous indignation or self-protection to bitterness and resentment. Revenge fantasies may start in your mind. You may begin to experience physical ailments. You'll end up with broken relationships. These are clear indications that something needs to be resolved.

Deciding with Determination

One married couple I know committed to "not letting the sun go down" on their anger. The husband wrote, "There have been many times we've been tempted not to resolve our conflict. But we forced ourselves to deal with it. My wife has been much better at it than I have been. I've struggled with wanting to get revenge. I'm so glad we made a promise to each other that we would, at all times, without exception, attempt to work it out. I think it has literally saved our marriage. It definitely is a big part of the reason our marriage is as strong as it is." This couple learned to resolve rather than run from their conflicts.

In chapter 13 we discussed the need to ask God for a desire to change, to make a personal decision to change our anger responses, to develop a detailed plan for doing so, and to follow through on the plan with determination—desire, decide, develop details, and be determined. If we don't do these things, we're bound to repeat our same mistakes over and over and over again. We need to commit to resolving our long-held, tightly gripped feelings. We need to acknowledge anger as the root of many of our problems and to realize how much it interferes with our relationship with God and our pursuit of godliness. We need to decide with teeth-clenching, firm-footed determination to resolve it, lest the enemy of our souls move in and take over.

> We need to decide with teeth-clenching, firm-footed determination to resolve it.

There are times when this takes more than determination. The wounds are so deep that major surgery is needed. The next chapter takes a further look at resolving deep anger—the deeply damaging kind that often seems beyond repair.

The Bottom Line

When angry, fight fair and don't let anger fester. Seek to resolve it as soon as possible. It may be painful, but the rewards are great.

Questions to Consider

1. Think of a situation in which you effectively resolved your anger over a person, place, or thing. What level of satisfaction did you find in that experience? Has that experience motivated you to improve your resolution skills? Why or why not?

2. What unresolved anger issue, if any, do you think most needs your attention right now? Do you feel uncomfortable, uptight, or infuriated whenever a certain person, place, or thing comes to mind? What steps can you take to put those feelings behind you?

3. What techniques for getting rid of anger have you found most helpful in this book?

Action Steps to Take

- List any areas of unresolved anger you are aware of in your life. Pray over each situation and for each person, place, or thing involved.

- Ask God what practical steps you should take toward resolving each of these anger wounds.

- Decide with determination to implement these steps toward resolution and share them with a trusted friend or mentor. If you are unaccustomed to taking some of the practical steps mentioned in this book such as keeping a journal, asking someone to hold you accountable, or praying with others, now would be a good time to start.

22

Resolving Deep Anger

It's hard to let go of anger—especially when its roots
are so deep and bitterness is in full bloom.

Resolving anger isn't easy. At times it can seem like an insurmountable, impossible task because the anger has grown
so deep. Is there any brewing and stewing inside of you? Is there
any place in your heart where the Holy Spirit could expose bitterness? Does something that happened or a particular person
(or persons) immediately come to mind? Does your blood pressure rise, your stomach churn, your heart pound, or your palms
become sweaty? Do you have a wound that immediately resur-
faces? An ex-mate, business partner, brother, sister, or parent?
Someone at work? A boss? A child? A grown child?

We've spoken to people who have been harboring anger for
many, many years—a man whose wife was killed in an accident,
a couple whose child died of a surgical complication, a woman
sexually abused over and over again, a businessman ripped off
by his partner, a woman whose husband was unfaithful, a grown
child who never felt loved and accepted by parents, and a person

whose spouse committed suicide. Perhaps you have a wound from a disagreeable neighbor, a rejecting friend, an abusive relative, an unappreciative boss, or domineering parents. Whatever happened, you find anger has become a permanent resident in your heart. If this is you, you need to deal with it now—for your own sake.

Consider the example of a young man who developed an infection from a rather superficial injury. He neglected to properly clean the wound and ignored the spreading infection. He developed gangrene and died—unnecessarily. If you and I allow anger to fester and become infected, it too can bring unnecessary and tragic death to our spiritual lives.

If you've been the victim of a severe offense or trauma—if your spouse was unfaithful, if you've been sexually abused, if someone close to you has committed suicide, or if anyone has otherwise caused you to suffer greatly—it only makes sense that you would be angry. In fact, you have a *right* to be angry. The problem is that having a right to be angry never really makes it better. If left unresolved, your anger can turn into a second problem. Then you will not only have to deal with the wrong someone did to you, you'll also have to deal with the wrong you've done to yourself.

> Having a right to be angry never really makes it better.

It may seem unfair that harboring anger about something you never would have chosen for yourself can actually do additional damage over and above the original event, but that's just the way life is. So go ahead and be angry for a while, and don't beat yourself up for having honest emotions. But eventually, for your own spiritual and emotional health, you'll need to deal with your anger. This chapter will begin to show you the way.

God can heal you of bitterness. Like a deep wound, it needs to be cleansed, treated, and bandaged. We'd like to suggest a three-part plan in dealing with the deep, unresolved anger that has festered in your heart:

1. Cleanse the wound of dirt and debris (Eph. 4:31).
2. Treat the wound with healing ointment (Eph. 4:32).
3. Bandage the wound for protection (Eph. 5:1–2).

Cleansing the Wound

My three sons and I (Chip) have gotten hurt a lot playing sports; we've had gashes, cuts, scrapes, strains, and sprains. Some have needed stitches and some splints. Many of our open injuries have been covered in mud or smeared with grass. In our frequent visits to the hospital emergency room, we've found the doctors and nurses to be painfully thorough in cleansing the wounds.

If you've ever experienced that, you know what it's like. As they dig deep inside the wound, you want to scream *"Stop!"* Just when you think they're done, they take a syringe filled with saline solution and pour it in the wound. If it's one of your children, you're thinking, "Oh God, help them!" Your stomach knots up. It hurts so bad to get the debris out. Then they do it again—three or four times. They want to thoroughly clean the wound. If you were to say, "Just pour a little of that stuff on and it'll be fine. Let's not do it so many times," the doctor would most likely give you one of those looks that says, "What, are you stupid? That could get infected!" Cleansing involves digging, scraping, swabbing, pouring, and disinfecting. It's not easy and painless. It's deep, thorough, complete—and not a whole lot of fun.

> God can heal you of bitterness. Like a deep wound, it needs to be cleansed, treated, and bandaged.

Dealing with anger is like that. It also begins with a thorough cleansing of the wound. It's not an easy, pain-free process, but it's essential if we want to fight off the infections that kill our soul. Once infected, we could put a bandage around our wounds or hide them, but our anger will still be there. The infection wouldn't go away by itself. So we have to get to the root of un-resolved anger. And with many of us, anger has cut deep down to the depths of our heart and requires major surgery.

Cleansing the wound means getting the debris out. Ephesians 4:31 tells us what the debris is: "Get rid of all bitterness, rage and anger, brawling and slander, along with every form of malice." God knows that this kind of debris leads to deadly infections.

The main reason anger doesn't get completely resolved is, as we've mentioned, our unwillingness and cowardice in facing the pain, acknowledging the debris, and asking God to clean it out. We hang on to our anger, slander others, wish them ill will, and we let it all turn to bitterness and rage. We wallow in anger's debris like a pig wallows in the mud. But how do we get rid of these infectious attitudes and actions? The answer: confess and repent.

You and I know that anger easily turns into bitterness, resent-ment, and malice. We can make excuses and recount the pain and hurt, but the bottom line remains: we must get rid of the infection and the debris, and clean our hearts. At some point we have to stop and say, "God, I admit that my response has been sinful. I repent of it. I want to lay it aside. I want my life to honor you." We confess our wrong and seek to turn around.

Living It Out

I (Chip) have a friend who was involved in an effective ministry until the day his wife decided to break her marriage vows and walk out on him. He lost his career and his family simultane-ously. The dreams and calling he was sure God had placed in him blew up in smoke. Not only that, his ex-wife embarked on a calculated smear campaign to keep him from his children and turn their hearts against him. A few months of manipulation, a court system sympathetic toward the tears of a pretty good ac-tress, and a web of deception later, the task was almost complete.

His precious children hardly knew him anymore, and what they thought they knew was based on lies. His life—everything he had hoped for—was in shambles.

It took my friend a very long time to get over his bitterness and despair. God was gracious to restore him and redeem his circumstances, but even today he sometimes has to remind himself that though the scars remain, those wounds are healed. There's always the tendency to wonder "what if . . . ," and then to fill in the blank with a much more ideal scenario of having made different choices or having foreseen problems far in advance. Those "what ifs" eat away at one's soul. For years this friend would feel rage whenever he thought of the injustice of the situation and the damage it had done to his kids. He knew in his heart that forgiveness was essential, but he wasn't in a very forgiving mood. He could say the words, but he couldn't overcome his anger or his regret—not without lots of prayer, some understanding friends and family, some wise counsel, and time. And, ultimately, not without the presence of God to comfort and rebuild.

The key, eventually, was repentance—not that of the offender but of the friend who held such bitterness in his heart. That's one of the subtleties of anger; it cultivates a victim mentality and portrays repentance always as someone else's responsibility. But true repentance is a willful turning from an action or an attitude, and it applies to anyone who harbors anger and bitterness. Those feelings have to be dealt with. They have to be confessed and then rejected. The one with a "right" to be angry has to learn how to walk away.

> That's one of the subtleties of anger; it cultivates a victim mentality and portrays repentance always as someone else's responsibility.

What about you? Do you have areas in which you need to confess and repent of harboring anger, rage, bitterness, and malice? What has your attitude been like since your ex walked out on you? What attitude have you had toward the business partner who ripped your life's work out from under you? What about the parent who abused you, who did not care for you, who didn't give you what you needed? How have you felt toward your ungrateful, blaming grown child? What is your attitude toward the boss or fellow employee who sabotaged your career and caused you to miss the opportunity of a lifetime?

Is it fair? No. Is it right? No. Should you act as if it didn't happen? Of course not.

The only way you cleanse the wound, however, is to get rid of all the debris and say to God, "Though what was done to me was wrong, though I'm really hurt and mad, I'm going to respond rightly—like Jesus."

We can't change what was done to us, but we can change our responses. If not, we live in a vicious cycle of unforgiveness and hurt. We develop heartburn, headaches, tension, and tight muscles. We develop and live in anger fantasies. We don't sleep. In the meantime, the people who offended us are sleeping well, enjoying vacations, dating other people, and going on with life. Our anger isn't eating them up; it's only gnawing at us. If we don't confess and repent, it will feast on the banquet of bitterness.

> **We can't change what was done to us, but we can change our responses.**

Here's a way to pray: "Lord Jesus Christ, I come before you confessing that I have allowed anger to fester inside. I ask you to forgive me and to help me get rid of those things I have done that dishonor you. You have forgiven me so much. Help me to forgive others and to let go of my ill will toward everyone against whom I've harbored it."

Treating the Wound

The second step toward getting rid of long, lingering anger is to treat the wound. Ephesians 4:32 commands us: "Be kind and compassionate to one another, forgiving each other, just as in Christ God forgave you." First we're told what to get rid of, and now we're told what to add on—kindness, compassion, and forgiveness, just like Jesus. God says that's how to treat a wound. You put on the antibiotic of forgiveness. It helps bring about healing. Forgiveness is both a command *and* a choice.

A Parable about Forgiving

Jesus told a story to help a group of people struggling with forgiveness (Matt. 18:23–35). He was explaining the aspect of divine forgiveness and told a parable, which in our day would perhaps be explained like this. One person owed another person about twenty million dollars. When brought before the man who owed the money, the debt-ridden man cried and prayed, "Please, please forgive me my debt." (In those days if you owed a debt, you went to prison where it was virtually impossible to pay it back.) The man, moved by pity, surprisingly responded, "I forgive you your debt."

As the debtor walked away, he came across someone who owed him money, a very small sum compared to what he had owed—about twenty dollars. The borrower begged the man, "Please forgive me my debt." Unlike the merciful man, he responded, "No way. Take him off to prison." Those who knew about the first debt being canceled were bothered by this and went back and told the forgiving man, "Hey, boss, you can't believe what happened. You know the guy whom you just forgave twenty million dollars? One of his slaves owed him twenty bucks, and he sent him to prison."

He said, "Call that guy back in here. I think we need to have a little talk." Then we read, "'Shouldn't you have had mercy on your fellow servant just as I had on you?' In anger his master turned him over to the jailers to be tortured, until he should pay back all he owed." Jesus ended the parable with a sobering point: "This is how my heavenly Father will treat each of you unless you forgive your brother from your heart."

If we listed every sin in our lives, every attitude and action that has violated the will of God, it would be fair to say that all of us have at least a twenty-million-dollar debt to God. But Jesus paid our debt on the cross, and God declares us forgiven. When we get an irate phone call, when we get ripped off, when we get emotionally scarred, we are to forgive. Whether set up or upset, we are to forgive.

Forgiving

God has forgiven us so much! How dare we not turn around and be merciful and forgiving to others? We are not to retaliate, rebut, or rebuke; we are not to dispute, disagree, or deny; we are not to fume, fester, or feud; we are to forgive.

The consequences of not forgiving are harsh: we will become prisoners to our anger. Will Rogers said, "I won't give any man the power over my life by me being angry at him." Anger drains our emotional strength. It robs us of joy and peace.

> "I won't give any man the power over my life by me being angry at him."—Will Rogers

We know the potential problems of not forgiving, but what are the benefits of forgiveness? In the in-depth, research-oriented book *To Forgive Is Human*, we read, "Forgiveness yields good things— peace, happiness, health, reconciliation.... People who forgave also tended to have fewer mental problems.... [Research supports] the power of forgiveness to heal the mind, body and spirit." The authors conclude that "correlational studies suggest that adopting a forgiving lifestyle is indeed related to reductions in anger."[1]

Forgiveness is choosing to release the hurt and the desire to pay back the person(s) who hurt us. It means that we willfully

> Forgiveness is choosing to release the hurt and the desire to pay back the person(s) who hurt us.

choose not to bring this up to God, to another person, or even in our own meditations. Forgiveness is saying, "I release the person from any further obligation or debt. I choose not to hurt the person who has hurt me. I refuse to nurse a grudge in my heart." And it's a choice, not a feeling. On a day-to-day basis, it means that I won't mention it again to the offender or to others—not in phone conversations, in letters, during little coffee talks, nor on any other occasion, no matter how easy the opportunity to do so. Every time it comes up, I'm going to deal with it myself.

Forgiveness, then, is an act of the will by faith. Though our hurt feelings may linger, we nevertheless commit to forgive. We must remember to be true to our faith, not our feelings. When painful feelings come up, we say, "God, I'm feeling that pain again. But I confess and repent of my unforgiveness and reaffirm my decision to forgive." We've found it helpful to write this decision down and date it—perhaps in the margin of your Bible or in your journal. We say to the Lord, "I want to continue to release that to you." In the beginning, you may have to do that fifteen or twenty times a day, but eventually, if you don't give up or give in, you'll be

> We must remember to be true to our faith, not our feelings.

able to forgive. When I find angry thoughts returning, I squelch them by saying aloud in a commanding voice, *"Forgiven!"*—as if proclaimed and pronounced by a powerful judge.

PRAY

How do we do it? Where do we begin the process of forgiving someone who has caused us such deep hurt? We begin with prayer. We need to get with God and ask him to give us the willingness to forgive. After lunch with my friend, I got out of the car, walked up to my office, shut the door, put my feet on my desk, and said, "God, I don't want to forgive this guy. I want him to pay." And then I said, "But God, will you create in me a heart that's willing to forgive? I don't have any right to harbor anger and unforgiveness after what you've done for me. Please help me."

Pray, asking God to help you have a willing heart. Ask God to create a growing desire within to forgive, to release the clingy anger that's stuck like superglue. The word *forgive* literally means "to loose." Ask God to loosen your desire for revenge.

DEVELOP EMPATHY

Another helpful approach is to seek to understand the other person's mind, motives, and emotions. The earlier researchers on forgiveness[2] encourage us to develop empathy—an understanding of the position, place, and feelings of the person who hurt us. We are to step inside their shoes, attempting to view the situation from their perspective, to think it through from their angle, to see what they were going through.

Have you ever had an experience in which someone treated you rudely and you responded indignantly (either inwardly or outwardly)—and then later you found out that their mate walked out on them that afternoon, or they'd just filed for bankruptcy the day before, or someone they loved was in a car wreck? All of a sudden, you think differently about how they treated you. *It doesn't excuse the behavior, but it does explain it.* And the offense no longer stings as much. Empathy makes it easier to forgive.

Cultivating empathy is essential on our path toward forgiveness. "Empathy is the plow that breaks up the hard ground of our hearts. The tenderness and compassion that follow empathy are seeds that sprout and grow until sworn enemies can sometimes surrender their hatred."[3] Research suggests that our ability to forgive is increased as we are able to empathize with those we view as responsible for our pain.[4]

Empathy is not only attempting to understand the offender's thoughts, feelings, and circumstances, it also involves a recognition of our own sinful nature, our own ability and propensity to hurt others. Just like the one who hurt us, we too are capable of hurting others in deeply painful ways. As I acknowledge my own dreaded deeds, failed friendships, and malicious mistakes, I gain perspective and can identify with my offender's humanity.

As my friend began to look at the spouse who walked away from him—her past relationships, childhood issues, problems, pressures, and feelings—the negative feelings loosened their grip on his heart and mind. He realized how she had learned to relate to people in dysfunctional ways and how he himself had said and done things that were painful to her. He still didn't agree with the way she handled the situation, but he could understand the emotions that motivated her actions. When we walk in another person's shoes long enough to get a sense of their perspective, needs, and hurts, we begin to develop a level of understanding that can bring about compassion instead of rage.

Empathy requires us to ask ourselves some important questions: Why did the person act this way? What was/is going on for them? What needs, values, or beliefs may have affected what they did? How have their past negative experiences perhaps contributed to their current behavior? What other problems or concerns may be affecting how they acted (health problems, disabilities, and inabilities)? When we take the time to answer these questions, much of our anger melts away.

Reconcile the Relationship

The third thing we need to do to extend and experience forgiveness is to seek reconciliation. With reconciliation, God asks us to go the second mile and seek, if possible, to restore the relationship with those who hurt or offended us.

Restoring a broken relationship may require that we step outside our comfort zone. It may involve confrontation and clear communication, as well as relinquishing the right to respond. The relationship may never be the same or have the same intensity level, but it probably won't be as prickly or rough around the edges. Even in the most contentious, strident relationships, like the kind ex-spouses often find themselves in, restoration is possible. It doesn't mean ever agreeing with that person or accepting what they did, but a good-faith effort to move beyond past conflicts can take all the sharpness out of it.

> **Restoring a broken relationship may require that we step outside our comfort zone.**

Reconciliation may involve dealing with the person face-to-face, making a phone call, or writing a letter (which we discussed in the chapter on Anger ABCDs). In the situation I (Chip) shared in the last chapter about the person who secretly recorded my conversation, I had my letter to him in my briefcase for over a year and then decided it needed to be tossed—not in the mail, but in the circular file beside my desk. But writing the letter helped me to get it out and give it to God. Write a letter stating that you have forgiven the person, then stick it somewhere until you can send it with genuine feelings of forgiveness.

Perhaps you need to make a phone call. While doing a study on forgiveness, God convicted me of unforgiveness. Many years ago, I felt deeply betrayed by a friend. Our paths took us in different directions. Though our contact ceased, the anger I felt did not. In my perspective, this person had been the cause of extreme emotional pain in my life. I yearned for him to ask me for forgiveness, but as I prayed one day, God called me to ask *him* for forgiveness.

At first I thought God didn't understand. I wanted him to help me forgive the guy who offended me. Instead, he said I needed to ask him to forgive me for harboring such anger, ill will, and resentment toward him all these years. As I confessed to God my unforgiving spirit, he revealed my own blatant sinfulness. Like the debtor in Jesus's parable, I had committed perhaps a greater sin. It was one of the hardest phone calls I've ever made, but the results were remarkable. I no longer cringe at the mention of his name. I no longer feel tense, uptight, and fragile when my memory journeys to that part of my life. I'm forgiven. I *have* forgiven. And I'm free.

You may be called to deal with the person face-to-face. It's extremely hard to go the second mile and extend forgiveness to someone you feel doesn't deserve it. You may be thinking, "Oh no, I can't do that!" But this is something you can't afford *not* to do. If it's still coming to your mind, if it's still eating you up inside, if you still feel distant in the relationship, it hasn't been dealt with. Sometimes God wants us to have a face-to-face. We need to be under control, loving, and clear. "I just want you to know, when this happened or when you said this, it really hurt my feelings. I'm not even sure you're aware of it. And I want you to know I forgive you."

As you've read in previous chapters, there are times when it's best to deal with the situation on your own. Writing a letter, making a phone call, or talking with the offender in person just causes the hurt feelings to escalate on one or both sides. If your feelings grow, then you know you weren't ready or that you had unspoken expectations about how the confrontation should go. And if the other person blows up, shuts down, blames others, or makes excuses, he or she wasn't ready or had unspoken expectations. It's better just to let it go.

It's also best not to deal with the person when it jeopardizes your job or other relationships. You may not be ready to lose your job over this thing. Deal with it and drop it. "God, I put it into your hands. I've done all I can. I'm not running from reconciliation. It just doesn't seem to be right to deal with the person directly now."

What Forgiveness Is Not

As we talk about forgiveness, it's important that we understand what it is and what it isn't. It's too easy to get stuck in misconceptions and foggy thinking about what it means to forgive. In their book *Seven Keys to Spiritual Renewal*, Stephen Arterburn and David Stoop provide a list of what forgiveness is not:

It is not condoning the behavior.
It is not forgetting what happened.
It is not restoring trust in the person.
It is not agreeing to reconcile.
It is not doing the person a favor.
It is not easy.[5]

It is, however, an attempt to let the past lie in the past and an agreement not to bring old offenses up again and again. Forgiveness may not make all relationships completely satisfying, but it has tremendous power to neutralize the volatile nature of even the worst of them. And with surprising frequency, it results in a supernatural ability to have compassion where anger and hatred once reigned.

Bandaging the Wound

The last step after the painful cleansing and forgiveness treatment is to bandage the wound. What do we mean by this? In Ephesians 5:1–2 we read, "Be imitators of God . . . and live a life of love, just as Christ loved us and gave himself up for us."

If you thought it was hard and radical before, watch out. This step produces plenty of dropouts. In order to put the past behind us, we must confess and repent (cleanse the wound) and forgive and seek reconciliation (treat the wound); but we are also called to love and bless those who have wronged us (bandage the wound). An "imitator of God" lives a life of love—with Christ as the example. As Jesus has unconditionally loved and mercifully forgiven us, we are to do the same.

Our ability to deal with anger is one of the most powerful weapons in God's arsenal for individual righteousness, corporate righteousness, and cultural change. We will never do anything as radical, as loving, or as Christlike than treating our enemies, real or perceived, graciously and mercifully. They may not deserve it, but then, neither do we. We are to be forgiving and reconciled, just as God in Christ forgave and reconciled us.

We go beyond our attitudes, beyond extending forgiveness, and beyond attempting reconciliation. God's way of truly putting the pain behind us requires that we bless those who have offended us. "Love your enemies, do good to those who hate you, bless those who curse you, pray for those who mistreat you" (Luke 6:27–28). Hating brings dissension; loves brings forgiveness (Prov. 10:12).

Every time I take the Lord's Supper, I lift up in prayer those who have offended me. I remember what Christ did for me unjustly. There was one person I prayed for every time we took the Lord's Supper for over a two-year period. "Bless him, God. Encourage him, enrich his marriage, cause good things to come into his life." For the first year, I always added, "and help him see the error of his way." But then I realized that my motives were impure.

Here's the entire scriptural admonition:

I tell you who hear me: Love your enemies, do good to those who hate you, bless those who curse you, pray for those who mistreat you. If someone strikes you on one cheek, turn to him the other also. If someone takes your cloak, do not stop him from taking your tunic. Give to everyone who asks you, and if anyone takes what belongs to you, do not demand it back. Do to others as you would have them do to you.

If you love those who love you, what credit is that to you? Even sinners love those who love them. And if you do good to those who are good to you, what credit is that to you? Even sinners do that. And if you lend to those from whom you expect repayment, what credit is that to you? Even sinners lend to sinners, expecting to be repaid in full. But love your enemies, do good to them, and lend to them without expecting to get anything back. Then your reward will be great, and you will be sons of the Most High, because he is kind to the ungrateful and wicked. Be merciful, just as your Father is merciful.

Do not judge, and you will not be judged. Do not condemn, and you will not be condemned. Forgive, and you will be forgiven. (Luke 6:27–37)

We can impact our world. We can transform our homes, our cities, and our country when we get mad about evil and injustice. But we'll need to have our own wounds healed before we can go out and do that. And chances are, we're going to get wounded in the process and need more healing along the way.

Romans 12:16–21 commands us:

- "Live in harmony with one another. . . . If it is possible, as far as it depends on you, live at peace with everyone."
- "Do not take revenge, my friends, but leave room for God's wrath, for it is written: 'It is mine to avenge; I will repay,' says the Lord. On the contrary: 'If your enemy is hungry, feed him; if he is thirsty, give him something to drink. In doing this, you will heap burning coals on his head.'"
- "Do not be overcome by evil, but overcome evil with good."

As far as it depends on us, we are to live in harmony and at peace with one another. We are not to harbor anger, take revenge, or retaliate with evil intent. Though we may yearn for revenge, we are not to pay back the hurt we've received. And here's a good test to see if we've really bandaged our wounds and moved on. Are we able to give, help, and serve those who have hurt us? ("If your enemy is hungry, feed him; if he is thirsty, give him something to drink.") Are we able to give up anger fantasies and our desire for revenge? Can we let God settle the score in his way and in his time, not ours? Can we wish them well? Can we say from our heart, by an act of God's grace, that we want this person's life, ministry, and family to be blessed? Can we truthfully say that there are no hard feelings anymore? It's hard and it takes time for the healing to occur, but the pain from cleansing, treating, and bandaging our wounds is nothing compared to the glorious freedom we feel and the worship and service we are able to give to God.

The Bottom Line

Below is a helpful summary of what we need to do to heal our deep wounds.

Resolving Deep-Seated Anger

What	Verse	Command	Steps
Cleanse	Ephesians 4:31	Get rid of bitterness, anger, malice, slander.	Confess and repent. Follow Christ's example: do not retaliate, entrust yourself to him who judges justly (1 Peter 2:19–21, 23).
Treat	Ephesians 4:32	Be kind, tenderhearted.	Forgive: 1. Pray. 2. Develop empathy. 3. Seek reconciliation.
Bandage	Ephesians 5:1–2	Be imitators of Christ.	"Live a life of love." "Love your enemies. Do good to those who hate you. Bless those who curse you. Pray for those who mistreat you" (Luke 6:27–28).

Questions to Consider

1. Think of the person toward whom you feel angry. What fears or obstacles stand in the way of your forgiving that person? Why has it been hard to get past those fears and obstacles?

2. Now that you have finished this book, what next step would help you the most to begin a lifestyle that deals effectively with the anger issues in your life?

3. What friend, small group, or process (i.e., journaling, practicing the ABCDs, etc.) do you think will be required for these principles of anger resolution to become an integral part of your life?

Action Steps to Take

Below are three very big assignments. They will take time and courage. You will likely find yourself reviewing various sections of the book in order to put them into practice. Don't be discouraged, and don't assume that your steps of obedience will cause others to do the same. Anger issues go deep into the heart and may well be the springboard to God doing some of the most significant work that you've ever experienced in your life and relationships. For this reason we highly suggest that you answer the following questions in the company of a friend, mentor, or small group of like-minded people.

- List those who have hurt you, and identify when and how they hurt you.
- List those whom you've hurt, and identify when and how you hurt them.
- Pray through each list, asking God to help you confess, repent, forgive, and love.

23

Anger's Higher Purpose

He that would be angry and sin not must not be
angry with anything but sin.

—Thomas Secker

The old story of the prince and the pauper tells of a prince
who has grown tired of a life of royalty, and a pauper who
dreams of living in a palace. The prince looks out over the palace
walls and wonders what it's like to live out in the city; the pauper
looks into the palace gates and wishes he could live inside. One
day they meet by chance and are struck by their similar appearance. They decide to trade places.

While posing as the prince, the pauper is served nuts. In order
to crack them, he uses a tool that he finds hidden away in the
palace. Little does he know that the heavily-weighted gold tool
is actually the king's official business seal. Without it, royal business cannot be conducted. Whenever he is served nuts, he uses
the seal to crack them, not knowing it is actually intended for a
higher purpose. The palace officials probably thought the prince
was, well, going nuts.

This is much like the way in which we tend to respond to and use anger. Anger is a God-given emotion that is intended to be used for a higher, greater purpose, but we often use it for other reasons.

Most of this book has focused on learning to control and contain destructive anger. We've read about being quick to hear, slow to speak, and slow to anger. We've learned about the different anger profiles. We agree that our relationships and lives improve as we learn to deal with anger effectively. The Bible gives us wonderfully helpful advice and commands on how to deal with anger.

As we learn to control our tempers, we become healthier emotionally. But that's not the only benefit. We are also called to be angry for good greater than just our own personal well-being.

Anger's Greater Good

If each of us were allotted a certain amount of anger fuel, close to 100 percent of it would be spent "cracking nuts"—getting angry about hurt pride, frustrations, and insecurities. But God gave us anger to use for his official business: "Defend the cause of the weak and fatherless; maintain the rights of the poor and oppressed. Rescue the weak and needy; deliver them from the hand of the wicked" (Ps. 82:3–4). How often do we get angry because of the injustices in the world, such as the maltreatment of people, the imbalance of global resources, genocide, war crimes, and religious persecution? Anger can motivate us to act on behalf of those who have been treated unfairly and unjustly. We are encouraged to "speak up for those who cannot speak for themselves, for the rights of all who are destitute. Speak up and judge fairly; defend the rights of the poor and needy" (Prov. 31:18–19).

Most of this book has focused on how to deal with *our* anger, but we must also learn how to experience and express God-motivated anger toward things outside of ourselves. Injustice, racism, drunk driving, molestation, abortion, abuse, assault, rape, partiality, elitism, murder, human trafficking, drug abuse, pornography, environmental devastation, and sexual exploitation are but some of the things that anger God.

When was the last time you got so mad that you were inspired to take action? When was the last time you wrote a letter, confronted someone, spoke out, or stood up? When was the last time you did something? When was the last time you responded, "That's not fair! Something's got to be done about that!"

Ninety-nine percent of us don't get mad about the things we ought to be mad about. Unless we are wronged personally, we sit back and apathetically accept it. Most of us can turn on the news and hear about murders, ill-treatment, idolatry, greed, genocide, and much more. Similarly, we can read the newspaper and get more emotional over the stock market, a new movie, or a good sale than we do over the tragedy, evil, and injustice that abound. We may think that these events are unfortunate, but they do not sink in deeply enough to inspire action. Have we become overwhelmed and grown numb to evil and injustice?

God wants us to move from using anger for primarily self-focused reasons to using it as it was really meant to be used. He wants us to be angry at things that anger him. This is anger's higher calling. As we develop constructive, God-guided anger, we learn more about the heart of God and what saddens and maddens him. We then begin to understand the depth of his love, patience, grace, and mercy.

The Commitment to Change

Do you remember Chip's weeding story? As a boy he mowed lawns and weeded gardens. At first he chose the easy way out with the weeds—he would take a pair of clippers, cut off the top, and be done quickly. But the weeds soon came back, and he'd have to cut them all over again. When he was willing to get his fingers dirty and dig down deeply, however, he was able to get the entire weed and didn't have to deal with it again.

This is what we need to do with anger. We need the courage, strength, and grace to face the root issues that bring anger, to get our fingernails spiritually and emotionally dirty and pull up things that may be painful. Through the Holy Spirit, God wants to deal with them once and for all.

God's advice and instruction on anger is timeless. Current and former approaches to anger management affirm God's wisdom and knowledge of our humanity. God also shows us how and when we should get angry. He challenges us to join in His indignation of wickedness. So take this as a challenge to make a commitment to change—to change old habits and patterns, to change what you say and how you say it, to communicate your needs clearly, to speak boldly against wickedness, and to stand up against injustice. Change can be hard, but God is there to help.

Appendix

———

Dealing with God's Anger at Us

There is yet another dimension to God's anger, which the Bible often refers to as "the wrath of God." God gets mad! He gets mad at injustice and evil, but he also gets mad at our individual sins. He gets mad at the things we do that hurt other people.

But God has resolved his anger by allowing Jesus Christ—fully God, fully man—to be the recipient of his anger. Romans 3 summarizes this: "There is no one righteous, not even one. . . . All have sinned and fall short of the glory of God and are justified freely by his grace through the redemption that came by Christ Jesus" (Rom. 3:10, 23–24). What good news! Because of Jesus, we can be forgiven.

God wants to heal our destructive anger, but more importantly he wants to heal us. He knows that controlling our anger is important, but also that letting him have control of our lives is even more important. Without him our lives spin out of control; he created us, loves us, and knows what is best for us. If you have not yet asked God to heal your hurts and forgive your sins, then perhaps you should consider praying something like the following:

Dear God, I'm sorry for the things I've done that make you angry. I ask you to forgive me. I believe that you placed your just anger on Christ instead of me because you love me. I want to be restored to you; please come into my life and make me the person you want me to be. Amen.

For those praying this prayer for the first time (or for those reaffirming God's role in their life), this is the biggest and most important step towards not only understanding anger, but also change that will last a lifetime.

Notes

Chapter 2: Understanding Our Anger

1. Lorrainne Bilodeau, *The Anger Workbook* (Center City, MN: Hazelden, 1992), 95.

2. Tim Jackson, *When Anger Burns* (Grand Rapids: RBC Ministries, 1994).

Chapter 3: Why We Respond the Way We Do

1. *American Demographics*, February 1998.

2. Bilodeau, *The Anger Workbook*, 19.

3. Harriet Lerner, *The Dance of Anger: A Woman's Guide to Changing the Patterns of Intimate Relationships* (New York: HarperCollins, 1997).

4. Bilodeau, *The Anger Workbook*, 10.

Chapter 6: Leakers

1. Quotation attributed to George Sala.

Chapter 9: Hurt from Unmet Needs

1. Joseph's life story is told in Genesis 37–50; the episode of his brothers' anger is found in chapter 37.

2. Bilodeau, *The Anger Workbook,* 69.

Chapter 10: Frustration from Unmet Expectations

1. Matthew McKay, Peter Rogers, and Judith McKay, *When Anger Hurts* (Oakland, CA: New Harbinger Publications, Inc., 1989), 80–81.

2. Hendrie Weisinger, *Anger Work-out Book* (New York: Quill, 1985), 108.

Chapter 12: The Anger ABCDs

1. Bilodeau, *The Anger Workbook*, 10.

Chapter 13: Anger Is a Choice

1. McKay, Rogers, and McKay, *When Anger Hurts*, 18.

Chapter 15: Step 2: Be Slow to Speak

1. Claudia Black, *Anger: A Blueprint for Twelve Structured Sessions* (MAC Publishing, 1996), 1–2.
2. Ibid.
3. Ibid.
4. McKay, Rogers, and McKay, *When Anger Hurts*, 132.
5. From Weisinger, *Anger Work-out Book*, 46.

Chapter 16: Step 3: Be Slow to Anger

1. McKay, Rogers, and McKay, *When Anger Hurts*, 149.

Chapter 17: Minimize Stress

1. John Ortberg, "Ruthlessly Eliminate Hurry," *Leadership Journal*, July 2002.
2. Carl Sandburg, "Anywhere and Everywhere People," *Complete Poems* (New York: Harcourt, 1950).
3. Tim Hansel, *When I Relax I Feel Guilty* (Colorado Springs: David C. Cook, 1979), 84–85.
4. Orin L. Crain in ibid., 9.
5. McKay, Rogers, and McKay, *When Anger Hurts*, 69.
6. Ibid., 197–98.
7. Alan Loy McGinnis, *The Friendship Factor* (Minneapolis: Augsburg, 1979).

Chapter 18: Maximize God

1. Weisinger, *Anger Work-out Book*, 202–4.
2. Paul Tournier, *Guilt and Grace* (San Francisco: Harper & Row, 1962), 160.

Chapter 19: Express Anger

1. John Stott, *The Message of Ephesians* (Downers Grove, IL: InterVarsity Press, 1979), 185.

Chapter 20: Express Anger Appropriately

1. Details from MADD's website, www.madd.org.

2. Mark Galli's *Jesus Mean and Wild* (Grand Rapids: Baker Books, 2006) explores this side of Jesus's character and reveals what is to many a surprising portrait of our Savior.

Chapter 21: Resolve Anger

1. Tim Jackson, *When Anger Burns*.

2. Chris Tiegreen's *Violent Prayer* (Sisters, OR: Multnomah, 2006) addresses this topic and urges believers to aggressively pray for God's kingdom to be made manifest wherever Satan has gotten a foothold.

Chapter 22: Resolving Deep Anger

1. Michael E. McCullough, Steven J. Sandage, and Everett L. Worthington, *To Forgive is Human: How to Put Your Past in the Past* (Downers Grove, IL: InterVarsity Press, 1997), 190, 191, 196, 197.

2. Ibid.

3. Ibid., 223.

4. Ibid., 141.

5. Stephen Arterburn and David Stoop, *Seven Keys to Spiritual Renewal* (Carol Stream, IL: Tyndale House Publishers, 1998).

Chip Ingram is the president and teaching pastor for Living on the Edge, an international teaching and discipleship ministry. His passion is to help everyday Christians actually "live like Christians" by raising the bar of discipleship. A pastor for over twenty years, Chip has a unique ability to communicate truth and winsomely challenge people to live out their faith. Chip is author of ten books, including *God: As He Longs for You to See Him*; *The Invisible War*; and *Love, Sex, and Lasting Relationships*. Chip and his wife, Theresa, have four children and six grandchildren and live in Georgia.

Becca Johnson, PhD, is a writer and speaker and has been a licensed psychologist for twenty years. Her life's work is to help people overcome negative experiences and emotions in order to more fully enjoy God's love. The author of books on guilt and child abuse, Dr. Johnson conducts counselor training in ten different countries and is currently in private practice in Washington state, where she lives with her husband, Lloyd, and their four children. The Johnsons have also served overseas as missionaries.

Jim Collins's *Good to Great* became a bestselling business book because it studies the characteristics of great businesses. But should Christians want to become great in the eyes of the world? In *Good to Great in God's Eyes*, bestselling author Chip Ingram shows how Christians can honor God with lives of great faith and excellent work. Believers become great in God's eyes by applying the ten common characteristics of great Christians:

- think great thoughts
- read great books
- pursue great people
- dream great dreams
- pray great prayers
- take great risks
- make great sacrifices
- enjoy great moments
- empower great people
- develop great habits

Using Scripture, personal stories, and examples from Christians who left a lasting legacy, Ingram offers practical steps for becoming great in all areas of life—including spiritual growth, family, relationships, and career.

"Chip Ingram poses the provocative question: 'Can greatness be a Christian calling?' And if it is, what are the most helpful practices of people who aim to be great in God's eyes? With his trademark combination of winsomeness and intensity, Chip answers these questions in a way that is both helpful and challenging. *Good to Great in God's Eyes* is timely, thoughtful, and biblical—all hallmarks of Chip's writing and teaching."

—**FRANK WRIGHT**, PhD, president and CEO, National Religious Broadcasters

How would you describe your best friend? Your spouse? Your children? When we know people well, our descriptions of them are richer and fuller than of those we know as mere acquaintances. So how would you describe God? And how does your view of God impact your life?

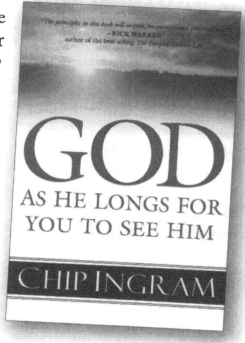

Join Chip Ingram in this fascinating study of seven attributes of God: his goodness, sovereignty, holiness, wisdom, justice, love, and faithfulness. You'll see God in a whole new light. It will change the way you pray, the way you live, and the way you think about the world around you.

God longs for you to know him as he really is.

Get ready to meet God again for the first time.

BakerBooks
a division of Baker Publishing Group
www.BakerBooks.com

Discover the secret to love that lasts.

Why do so many relationships go wrong?

At first, that true love seems perfect, the answer to
all your dreams. But with time and familiarity, the
tension mounts. You're disappointed and doubtful.
Before long, love crumbles and you're left alone or
stuck in a meaningless marriage.

But wait—it doesn't need to end that way.

A love relationship can be lasting and deeply
satisfying. It can be transformed from unhappy
drifting into intimate joy, filled with vibrant sex
and clear communication.

So what's the secret?

"There's a better way to find love, stay in love, and
grow in intimacy for a lifetime," says Chip Ingram.
It's God's way. With hope and certainty, he explains
how God's prescription for relationships creates a love that lasts. A love you can enjoy.

Whether single, single again, or wanting more from your marriage, you can begin the
delightful journey toward a lasting, loving relationship. This practical, insightful book will
show you how.

"To anyone hungering for a meaningful relationship, here is a trustworthy escort out of
our current confusion."

—Howard G. Hendricks, distinguished professor and chairman, Center for Christian
Leadership, Dallas Theological Seminary

"In the needs and the complexities of fulfilling relationships, Chip Ingram provides a
road map to success and deepening joy."

—Dr. Joseph M. Stowell, president, Cornerstone University

BakerBooks
a division of Baker Publishing Group
www.BakerBooks.com

VISIT YOUR LOCAL CHRISTIAN BOOKSTORE.

WHAT'S NEXT?

*Living on the Edge offers several small group studies at **LivingontheEdge.org**:*

r12: True Spirituality   *10 Week Study*

Being a genuine disciple of Christ flows out of a relationship with Him. It's about experiencing God's grace, not earning His love through performance. A real relationship with Jesus Christ will produce a follower whose life looks progressively more like His life. Romans 12 provides a relational profile of an authentic disciple. Christians who live out this kind of lifestyle are what we call r12 Christians. God is willing to go deeper and grow you into a real disciple... are you ready? Messages include: 1) God's Dream for Your Life Overview; 2) How to Give God What He Wants the Most; 3) How to Get God's Best for Your Life; 4) How to Come to Grips with the Real You; 5) How to Experience Authentic Community; 6) How to Overcome the Evil Aimed at You. Each DVD message is approximately 30 minutes of teaching.

Miracle of Life Change   *10 Week Study*

Is life change really possible? If we're honest most of us would answer, "No." You've tried numerous programs that promise big changes, but in reality, deliver very little results. You long for transformation, but don't know where to begin. There's good news for you and there is hope. This teaching from Ephesians makes life change possible! Each DVD message is approximately 30 minutes of teaching.

Effective Parenting in a Defective World   *9 Week Study*

Raising children is a tough challenge in today's world. Peers and pop culture exert a never-ending pressure on kids. Many come from split homes. But the good news is that God has been working with people from bad situations for a long time! Chip Ingram will lead you to a new understanding of how God's principles for raising children still work today. He also shares from personal experience as a father who has coped with teenage rebellion and other challenges. Packed with practical advice, this series will give struggling parents a vision for their children's future and life-changing help for today! Each DVD message is approximately 30 minutes of teaching.

Five Lies That Ruin Relationships   *10 Week Study*

Have you ever looked back over a circumstance or relationship in your life and wondered how it became so messy or difficult? In this series centered in the book of James chapters 4 and 5, we'll define five of the most common lies that have the potential to ruin relationships with those we love. We'll uncover the source of quarreling, how our words wound, how not to make decisions, and why better things don't always make things better. Together we'll ask and answer: do wrong beliefs produce wrong behavior? What we think about life determines how we live it. There is power in knowing and applying God's truth when confronted with these lies and discovering the freedom He longs for us to enjoy in our relationships. Each DVD message is approximately 30 minutes of teaching.

The Living on the Edge Community.

Over 40 Online Growth Resources + the r12 Online Experience...FREE!

It's jam-packed full of free audio & video resources from Chip Ingram and others to help make your faith real. You can watch, listen, download messages, and share with your friends.

All New Community Features
- Video Messages
- Audio Messages
- MP3 Downloads
- Community Blog
- Chip's Corner
- Resource Sharing

Grow Deeper with the r12 Online Experience
A new guided discipleship pathway from Living on the Edge based on Romans chapter 12.

All the Features You Remember & More
- Radio Offers
- Listen Online
- Radio Broadcasts
- Podcasts
- TV Broadcasts
- Message Notes

Join now to experience the New Living on the Edge Community & r12 online today!

LivingontheEdge.org

are you **r12?**

Being a genuine disciple of Christ flows out of relationship with Him. It's about experiencing God's grace, not earning His love through performance. Romans chapter 12 provides a relational profile of an authentic disciple. Christians who live out this kind of lifestyle are what we call r12 Christians . . .

- **surrendered** to God
- **separate** from the world
- **sober** in self-assessment
- **serving** in love
- **supernaturally** responding to evil with good

God is willing to go deeper and grow you into a real disciple... Are you ready?

to get r12 resources or learn more, go to LivingontheEdge.org today!

r12 media resources
- dvd series
- cd series
- study guide

the r12 online experience...FREE!
- video Q&A
- life coaching
- interactive study
- online journal
- leader resources

r12
true spirituality™